Analyzing Performance Problems

or

'You Really Oughta Wanna'

BOOKS BY ROBERT F. MAGER

Preparing Instructional Objectives, Second Edition

Measuring Instructional Intent

Goal Analysis

Analyzing Performance Problems
(WITH PETER PIPE)

Developing Attitude Toward Learning

Developing Vocational Instruction
(WITH KENNETH M. BEACH, JR.)

BOOKS BY PETER PIPE

Objectives—Tool For Change

Analyzing Performance Problems
(WITH ROBERT F. MAGER)

Practical Programming
(HOLT, RINEHART & WINSTON)

Analyzing Performance Problems

or

'You Really Oughta Wanna'

by

ROBERT F. MAGER

and

PETER PIPE

1970

FEARON·PITMAN PUBLISHERS, INC.

Belmont, California

ISBN-0-8224-0301-3

Library of Congress Catalog Card Number: 73–140896.

Printed in the United States of America.

Preface

Solutions to problems are like keys in locks; they don't work if they don't fit. And if solutions aren't the right ones, the problem doesn't get solved.

This book is about problems that arise because someone isn't doing what he is supposed to be doing or what you would like him to be doing. It describes each of a series of questions to ask when faced with this sort of "performance problem," and offers a quick-reference checklist to help you determine what sort of solution is most likely to work.

If you have ever been told, or have said, "We've got a training problem," or "They could do it if they wanted to," this book will help.

Contents

CHAPTER 0

Considering the Whole

People don't do things for zillions of the darnedest reasons, leading to all sorts of problems. And when there *are* problems—caused by differences between what people do and what someone wants them to do—the common solutions are to inform or exhort, or both. We say, "I've got to teach him . . . ," or we proclaim, "He really must change his attitude . . . ." But people problems come in many guises. They are solved by different remedies. And the one who is best at analyzing the nature of the problem will be more successful at solving it.

You're in the presence of the kind of problem we're talking about when you hear statements such as:

"They're not doing it the way they're supposed to."
"They don't have the right attitude."
"Absenteeism is too high."
"We need a course to teach people to . . . ."
"We've got a training problem because our workers aren't safety conscious."
"My salesmen don't sell our products."
"We've got to teach our students to turn in their assignments on time."
"I don't know why my kids don't mind like they oughta."

It's a mistake to assume that the answer to any of these problems necessarily involves either information or exhortation. (And usually it's an even worse mistake to assume that transfer or terminate—the standard solution of so many supervisors—is automatically the answer.)

The trouble with all statements of the kind we've listed is that what people identify as "the problem" often isn't the problem at all. It is merely a symptom of the problem. Until the problem is understood in greater detail, proposing a solution is simply shooting from the hip.

"You Really Oughta Wanna" is about how to find solutions to problems of human performance. Sometimes the solution is to provide information; if he doesn't know, instruction is likely to help. But when a person does know how and still doesn't perform, you can teach or exhort until your socks fall off and not solve the problem.

In this book, we describe a procedure for analyzing and identifying the nature and cause of performance problems of this type. We will give you a series of questions for each step of the analysis, and we will provide a quick-reference checklist to help you determine which solution is most likely to work. Once familiar with the procedure, you will find it quick and easy to use. Not only that, but you may find yourself with a new problem—learning to tolerate what you now can see quite plainly (like a man with X-ray vision) are expensive misfits between existing problems and solutions.

Flow Diagram

We will describe the steps of the procedure one by one (how else?); and, so that you can see the sequence of steps and also keep track of where you are, we will center our discussion around a flow diagram (opposite). That calls for a cautionary note, though. The flow diagram makes it look as if everything is neatly welded into place and that each step leads inevitably to the next. *Don't be deceived by appearances.* The formula is not rigid. Some of the steps logically belong in the sequence we have depicted. Others are not so related, notably those on the right-hand side of the diagram. They are shown in what looks like a sequence simply because we can talk about only one thing at a time. When you come to apply them, you

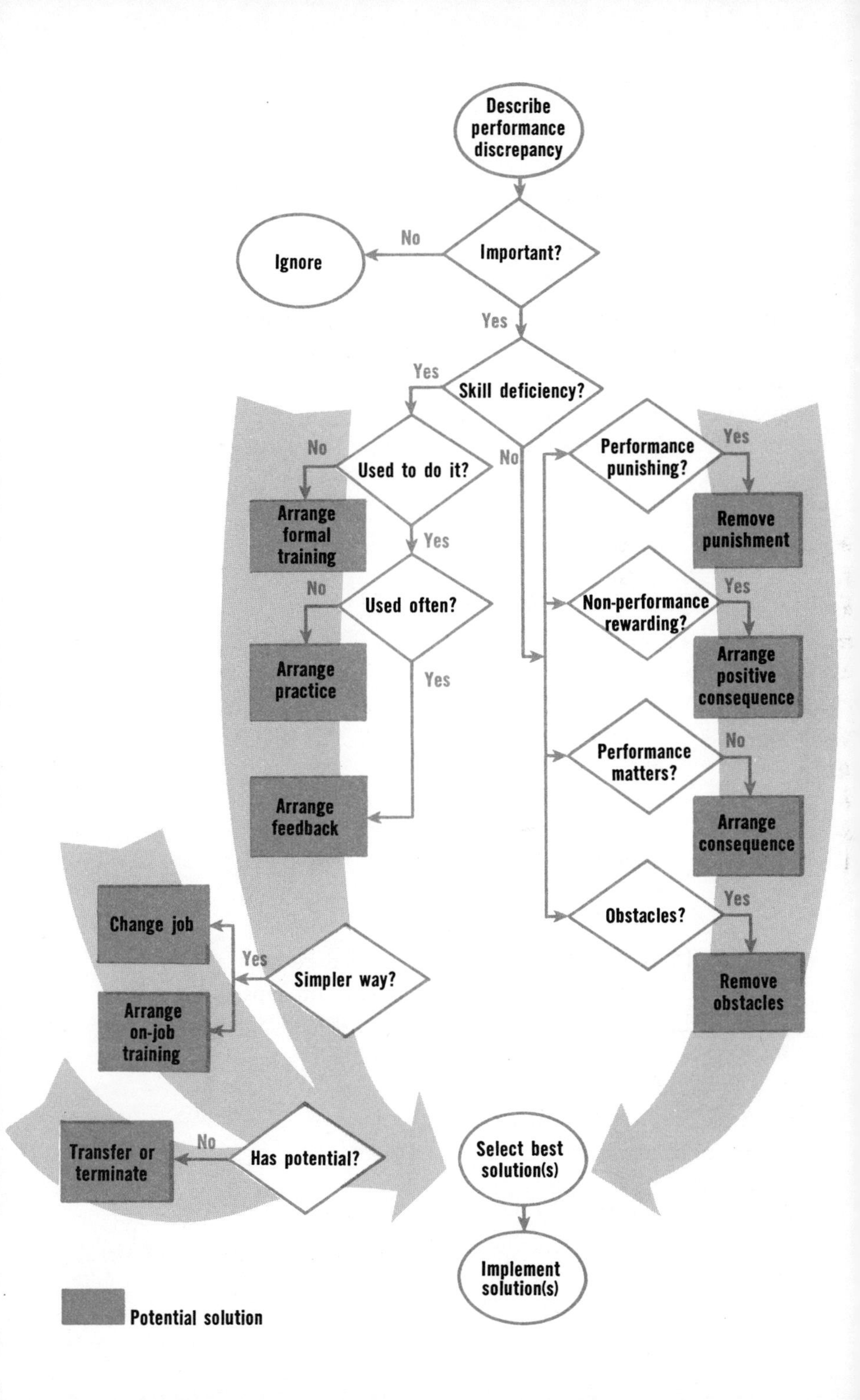
Describe performance discrepancy
Important?
No
Ignore
Yes
Skill deficiency?
Yes
Used to do it?
No
Arrange formal training
Yes
Used often?
No
Arrange practice
Yes
Arrange feedback
No
Performance punishing?
Yes
Remove punishment
Non-performance rewarding?
Yes
Arrange positive consequence
Performance matters?
No
Arrange consequence
Obstacles?
Yes
Remove obstacles
Change job
Yes
Simpler way?
Arrange on-job training
Transfer or terminate
No
Has potential?
Select best solution(s)
Implement solution(s)
Potential solution

may find that you can leap a step or two and go directly to the solution. The intuitive leap is fine. In fact, our whole approach is designed to tap your serendipity button as often as possible. That leads to yet another note of caution, however: Beware the hazards of considering only one possible solution to any problem. That's only one stage better than viewing all performance discrepancies as problems of training or attitude. To avoid this trap, you'll find the flow diagram and the checklist of questions in Part V useful. Run your problem through all the steps before you decide that your analysis is complete.

PART I

He Isn't Doing What He Should Be Doing.

I think I've got a training problem.

The procedure we are about to describe is one that shows you how to analyze the nature, the importance, and the cause of things called *performance discrepancies.* Since you can't analyze one unless you know one when you see it, let's begin there.

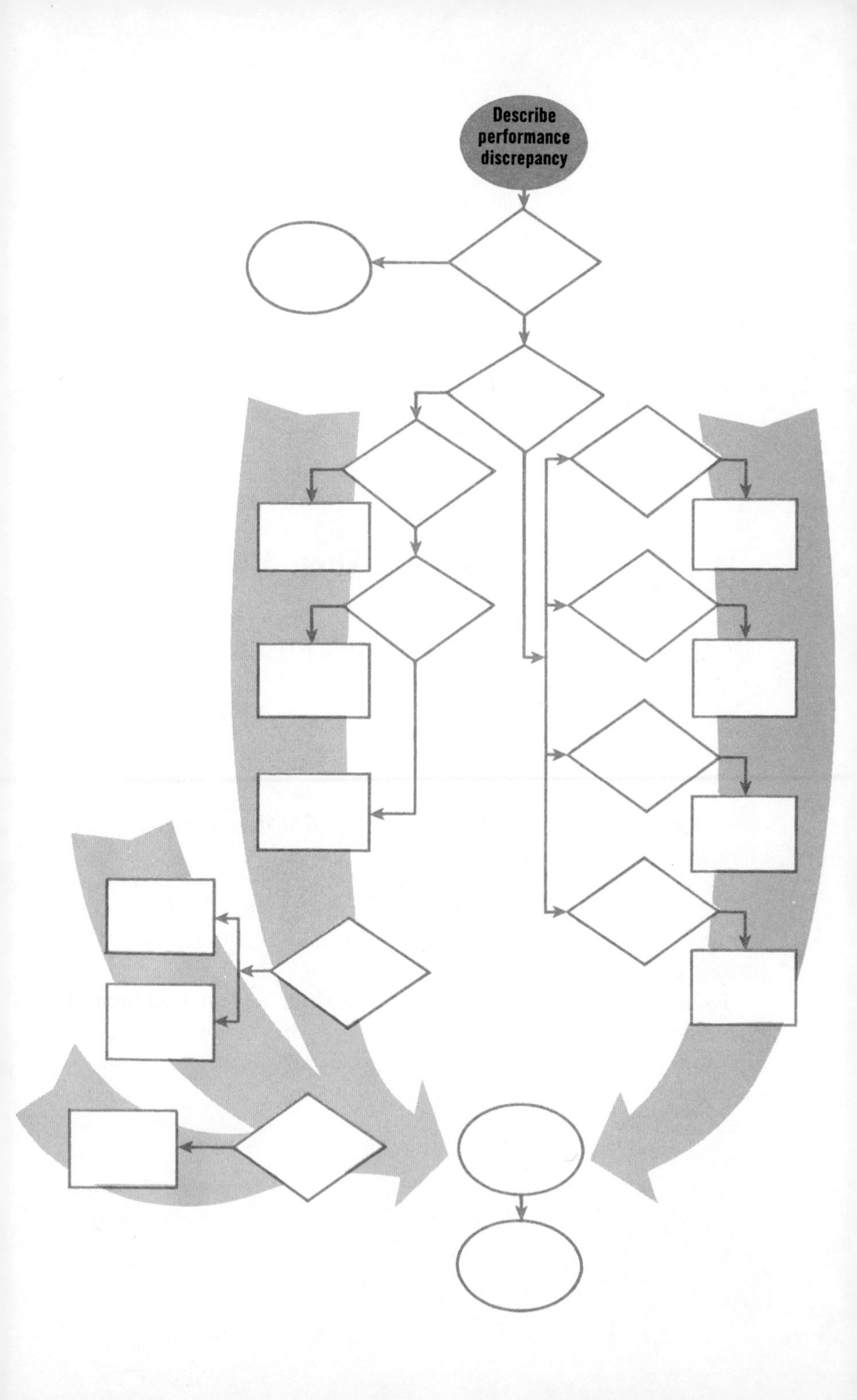
Describe performance discrepancy

CHAPTER 1

What Is the Performance Discrepancy?

■ WHERE WE ARE

We are considering the nature of a performance discrepancy.

Life is studded with discrepancies. There are discrepancies between what people tell us and what we know to be true, between what others believe and what we believe, between the things we want and our ability to pay—and any number of discrepancies between what *is* and what we would like it to be. One such discrepancy is that between someone's *actual* performance and his *desired* performance. This is a performance discrepancy, the kind of discrepancy with which we will be working.

Examples of performance discrepancies can be found all around us. Sometimes we get too little, sometimes too much. There's the typist who doesn't type accurately enough to suit you, the secretary who organizes your schedule to the point of bossiness; there's the son who doesn't wash the family car as often as promised, the mechanic who sells you an unneeded oil change; and there are the members of the congregation who don't show up regularly enough to suit the minister and the lady who is unnecessarily bossy with the altar guild.

Many of these discrepancies need not exist. Many of them can be eliminated.

As we stated in our Preface, one common occurrence that warns you that a performance discrepancy may be lurking around is the announcement that takes some form of "We've got a training problem." Someone has detected a difference between what is desired and what is actually happening.

But statements such as "We've got to train/teach . . . " are pits into which one can pour great amounts of energy and money unproductively. Such statements talk about *solutions,* not *problems.* Training (teaching, instruction) is a solution, a remedy—a procedure used to achieve desired results. It implies transferring information to change someone's state of knowing or ability to perform.

But lack of information is often not the problem. Let's take a couple of our earlier examples:

> "We've got a training problem because our workers aren't safety conscious."
>
> "We've got to teach our students to turn in their assignments on time."

Workers *know* they are supposed to follow safety precautions. Kids *know* they are supposed to turn in their homework assignments on time. And when someone *already knows* how to do what you want him to do, further instruction is not likely to get the results you want.

When someone says, "I've got a training problem," he's like the fellow who goes to his doctor and says, "I've got an aspirin problem." It's possible that aspirin will solve his problem; but aspirin is the solution, not the problem.

We are careful to use the word *discrepancy* rather than *deficiency.* "Discrepancy" means only that there is a difference, a lack of balance between the actual and the desired. "Deficiency" means that a value judgment has been made about a discrepancy, and that the discrepancy is bad or in some other way unacceptable. Using the word *discrepancy,* we avoid jumping to conclusions about whether a discrepancy is good or bad; and this way we remember to ask the questions that will give us a solid fix on the importance of the discrepancy.

To recognize a performance discrepancy, ask *why* it occurred to someone to say such things as: "I've got a training problem." "We need a course." "He needs a lesson." Or: "They oughta wanna be interested." And even: "Why can't they ever get it right?"

Each of these statements is only a symptom of a performance discrepancy, not a description of one. And the first step toward eliminating one is understanding its nature. It may be that you noticed people working slower than usual or slower than you desire. It may be that children are leaving more food than you think is reasonable, or that they are using unacceptable language. It may be that someone is less accurate or less careful than desired, or it may be an action as exasperating as that discovered by the manager of a motion picture distribution house—people "splicing" film with staples and scotch tape.

The first step is to ask yourself, "*Why* do I say something is not the way it ought to be? Why do I say there is a 'training' problem? What *event* causes me to say that changes must be made?"

What to do

Identify the *nature* of the discrepancy. Once the nature of the discrepancy has been identified, its importance can be considered.

How to do it

Ask these questions:

- Why do I think there is a training problem?
- What is the difference between what is being done and what is supposed to be done?
- What is the event that causes me to say that things aren't right?
- Why am I dissatisfied?

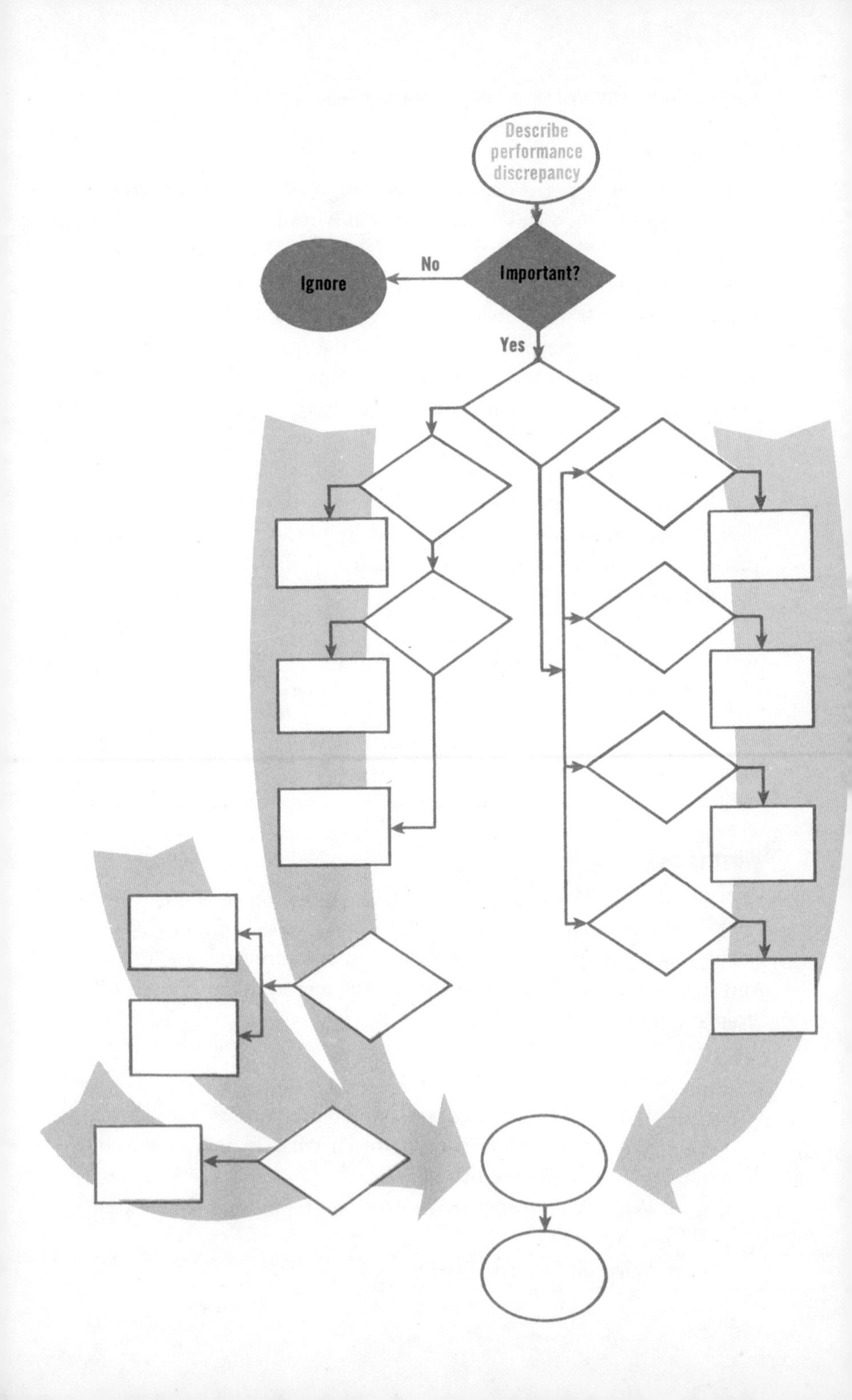
Describe performance discrepancy
Important?
No
Ignore
Yes

CHAPTER 2

Is It Important?

■ WHERE WE ARE

A performance discrepancy has been identified.

Sometime in the late 1960's, many businessmen began to find a discomforting discrepancy between what they wanted and what they were getting with regard to the length of young men's hair.

"They oughta be ashamed of themselves," said these businessmen. "We've got to teach them not to look like girls." (Translation: They should wear their hair the way *I* wear *my* hair.)

The discrepancy here was obvious: about three inches of hair. And it was identified and verbalized. But merely identifying a difference between what someone is doing and what you would like them to be doing is *not* enough reason to take action. So, at this point in the analysis procedure, it is well to ask whether the discrepancy is important enough to warrant further consideration.

When one manager was asked about the importance of his hair discrepancy, the conversation went like this:

"You are displeased with the length of the new employees' hair?"

"Yes. It is disgraceful."

"Aside from your displeasure with long-haired males, what would be the consequence of ignoring it?"

"What?"

"What would happen if you let it alone? What would happen if you ignored it?"

"Well, it probably wouldn't make much difference to business. But they ought to have more respect for the company. They ought not to want to look so sloppy." Translated, this means that there would be no serious consequence in terms of company success or failure. It means only that the shorthairs would continue to be made uncomfortable by the longhairs. In such a case, it is hardly worth the trouble, and probably unwarranted, to try to remove the discrepancy.

Other companies had a different answer, however. One machine shop foreman said: "Listen, buster. Nobody in my shop wears long hair . . . or long *anything*. Guys with long hair, or long ties, or loose clothing are a hazard to themselves and to others because they can get themselves caught in the machinery."

And another manager said: "Most of our customers are shorthairs. If we send them a longhair salesman, we just might be out of business."

In these cases there *is* a consequence of some importance, and action to eliminate the discrepancy is probably warranted.

Our example is intended to illustrate that not every discrepancy between what people do and what we would like them to do is worth trying to eliminate. It is simply not realistic to expect to be able to remold the world into an image of our own desires. We must be selective about which discrepancies to attack. The way to do that is to check the consequences of leaving the discrepancy alone.

A useful thing to do is to complete the sentence, "The discrepancy is important because . . . ." This will help you avoid (and help you help someone else avoid) the head-nodding that is so easy when the question is asked in the yes-no form. Completing the sentence will force into the open the reasons *why* someone says the discrepancy is important. Once that is done, the importance of the discrepancy can be evaluated more realistically.

WHAT WOULD HAPPEN IF YOU LEFT IT ALONE?

Many discrepancies often exist only in the eyes of the beholder. They are simply personal biases about what is "right" or a blind preference for "the way we've always done it." If you insist that a discrepancy is serious, be sure at least to ask, "Is it likely that the effort of searching for a solution will be justified by the results?"

The elimination of discrepancies can be approached from two directions. You can change what you are getting (the actual performance), or you can change your expectations (the desired performance). Or, of course, you can change both.

Changing the expectations is something that you can do on *your* side of the fence, and it may be the easiest way out. As far as the "performer" (the employee, the student, the child) is concerned, the effect is that the discrepancy has been ignored.

In summary, when you hear such statements as

"We've got to teach those kids to stop using teen-age jargon."
"My wife's cooking is getting worse instead of better."
"The percentage of defective products is still going up."
"Five percent of the medication given in this hospital is administered in error."
"The ties those darned mail boys wear are so loud you can hear them clear in the next county."
"Skirts are too short."
"Skirts are too long."

you are hearing the clarion call of someone perceiving a performance discrepancy. To keep from getting trapped into inappropriate and probably ineffective action, start asking questions. So far, the questions are:

1. What exactly is the discrepancy being described?
2. Is the discrepancy important?

What to do

Determine the importance of the discrepancy. If it is not important, ignore it. If it is important, proceed to the next series of steps aimed at determining the cause of the discrepancy.

How to do it

Ask these questions:

- *Why* is the discrepancy important?
- What would happen if I left the discrepancy alone?
- Could doing something to resolve the discrepancy have any worthwhile result?

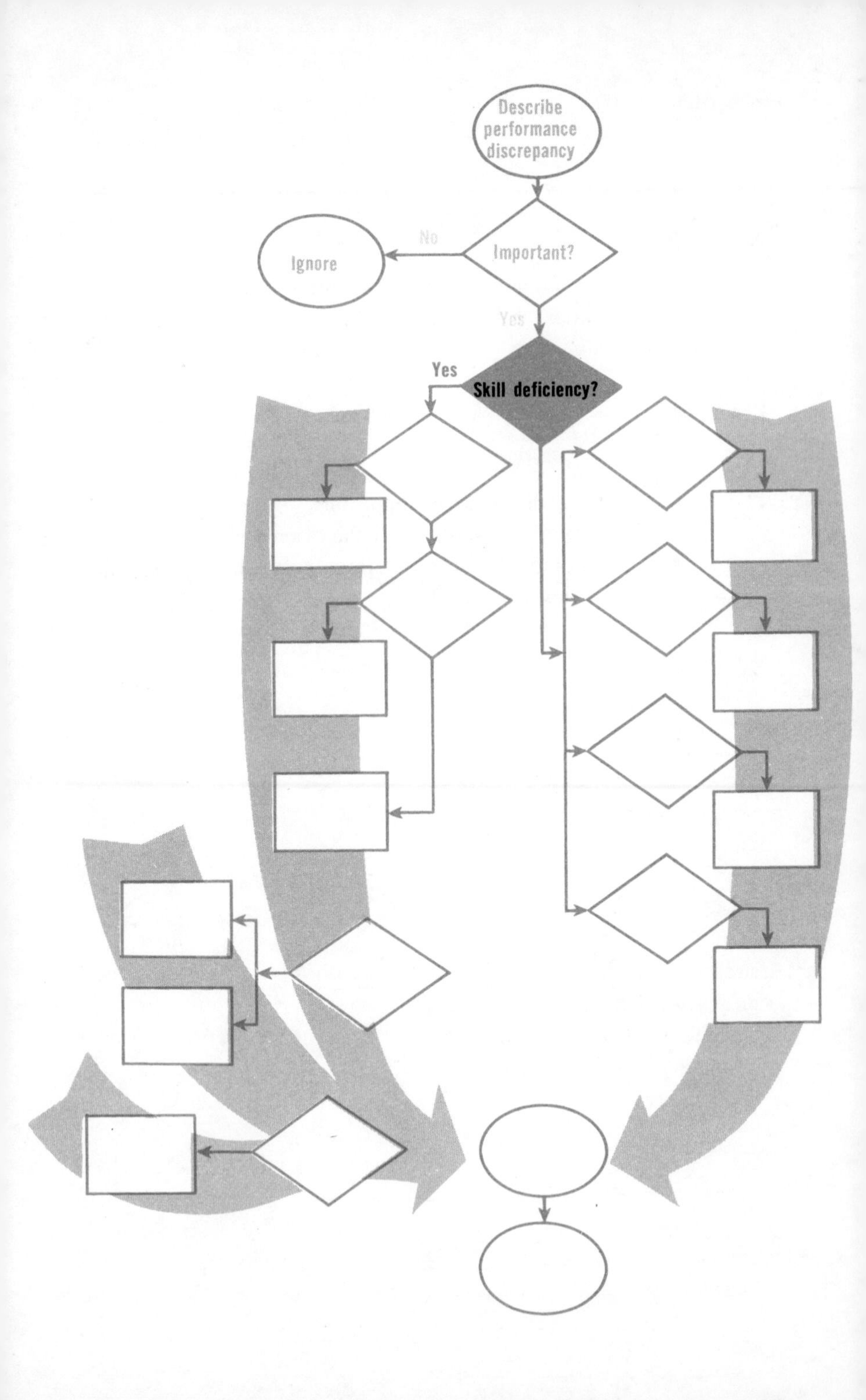

Describe performance discrepancy
No
Ignore
Important?
Yes
Yes
Skill deficiency?

CHAPTER 3

Is It a Skill Deficiency?

■ WHERE WE ARE

A performance discrepancy exists. It is considered important.

Now we begin to determine the *cause* of the discrepancy, so that an appropriate remedy can be selected or designed. This is a pivotal point in your checklist of questions, because the answer to this next question determines which of two sequences of questions you will follow.

In this step you must decide whether the performance discrepancy is due to a *skill deficiency*. In essence, is he not performing as desired because he *does not know how* to do it? If his life depended on it, would he still not perform?

If there is a genuine skill deficiency, then the primary remedy must either change his skill level (teach him how to do it) or change what is required of him.

If, on the other hand, he is able to perform but doesn't, the solution lies in something other than in enhancing his skills. "Teaching" someone to do what he already knows how to do isn't going to change his skill level. The remedy in these cases is to change the conditions under which he is expected to do that which he already knows how to do.

Here are some illustrations taken from life.

The manager of a medium-sized food company says, "I've got a training problem, and I want you to develop a training program to solve it."

We ask him to explain.

"In our new plant we make only six varieties of our product; and because we have only six varieties, our salesmen travel around in panel trucks with a supply of each. In a sense, each salesman is a traveling warehouse."

"And the problem?"

"The salesmen are pushing only *one* product instead of all six. I want you to teach them to sell all products equally."

"Do they know *how* to sell the other five?"

"Of course. It's no different from the one they are pushing."

"Do they know as much about those other five as they do about the one they're selling well?"

"Certainly they do. We have a good product course, and they have been carefully trained in all of the products."

"So they could sell the others if their lives depended on it?"

"Of course. But they don't."

"Do you have any idea why they don't push those other five products?"

"Well, yes. I suppose it's because they get three times as much commission for the one as they do for the other five. But they ought to want to sell the others *anyhow*."

Aha! What started out to be one of those "I've got a training problem" episodes turns out to be something entirely different. The performance discrepancy is clearly *not* due to a lack of skill. The salesmen *could* sell the products, but they don't. In this case, training is clearly not the remedy. What would you teach? What would you put into a course? What information could be imparted that the salesmen do not already have? True, you could lecture them on the importance of selling the products equally (if they don't already know that). Or you could explain how their jobs depend on their selling those other five products (if that is really true). But training will *not* make any difference in their *skill* at doing that which the manager wants them to do. Since they already know how to do as desired, the answer is not training. It's something else.

Another example: A principal says, "We've got to teach these kids not to write on the toilet walls."

Well, what would you put into a course on Non-toilet-wall Writing? Can't you just see the curriculum?

Monday. Introduction to Non-writing
Tuesday. History of Non-writing
Wednesday. Toilet Appreciation
Thursday. Famous Johns and Their Dastardly Defacement
Friday. Pot Power

Managers are often heard to say, "If only we could make these people more safety conscious." One interview with a manager went like this.

"Safety is a real problem for you?"

"Yes, it is. Every year we lose two million dollars because of accidents."

"Do you think your employees can recognize a safety hazard when they see one?"

"Oh, sure. Most of them have been around for some time, and they know what's safe and what isn't."

"Do they know how to report a safety hazard?"

"Yes, but they don't. And they oughta wanna do more about safety. It's in their own best interest. We need to teach them to be more safety conscious."

So the manager put safety posters on the walls, and he insisted that his people watch safety films regularly.

Nothing much happened to the accident rate, as might be expected, for this was another of those cases where people knew how to perform as desired but didn't. It was another of those cases where there existed an important performance discrepancy that was *not due* to a skill deficiency. In such cases the question is not one of what to teach, but rather one of how to rearrange things to get the performance that is already available.

At this point we will take a closer look at a term we will deliberately be using throughout the book—"oughta wanna." This is the key term to look for when trying to determine whether a performance discrepancy is due to a lack of skill.

Whenever you hear someone say, "He oughta wanna," or some variation thereof (usually accompanied by the waggling of a forefinger), it is almost certain that you are *not* dealing with a skill deficiency. It is almost certain that the person *could* perform as desired if the conditions and the consequences were right.

- The salesmen know how to sell the products, but they don't; they oughta wanna.
- Kids oughta wanna brush their teeth without being nagged.
- George oughta wanna clean his shoes before coming into the house.

No amount of information, no amount of exhortation, is necessarily going to change an "oughta wanna" situation. What's needed is a change in the conditions or the consequences surrounding the desired performance. "You oughta wanna do it *for your own good*" is not a potent motivator; it is one of the weakest techniques known for influencing anyone to do something he already knows how to do.

In thinking about this issue, we wonder if the trouble doesn't spring from the imprecision with which we so often use our language. We say things like, "I'll *teach you* to sass your mother." But this does not mean that the speaker intends to instruct the sasser in how to sass the sassee. It means that the speaker intends, through the arrangement of conditions and consequences (whap!), to modify the performance of the sasser—to cause him to do something he already knows how to do; namely, refrain from sassing.

Perhaps this explains the genesis of the expression "I've got a training problem." It seems that whenever we see a difference between what someone is doing and what we would like him to be doing, we conclude that the way to get the difference reduced is by training, by instruction. But training is only one of the remedies for a performance discrepancy. In fact, training is only one of the remedies *even when* a genuine skill deficiency exists.

In summary, then, when you detect an important performance discrepancy, it is *not* automatically a "training problem" and the solution does not necessarily involve teaching/training. Before you can arrive at a true solution (one that works, that is), you must first discover what kind of problem you have. And the key step in this is to determine whether the performance discrepancy is due to a genuine skill deficiency.

We'll consider first the case in which *a skill deficiency does exist.* Part II will lead you through the appropriate path on the flow diagram. Then, in Part III, we will back up to the same choice point and describe the path followed when the skill is there but the performance is not.

What to do

Determine whether the discrepancy is due to a genuine skill deficiency.

How to do it

Ask these questions:

- Could he do it if he really had to?
- Could he do it if his life depended on it?
- Are his present skills adequate for the desired performance?

PART II

Yes. It Is a Skill Deficiency.

He couldn't do it if his life depended on it.

We're face to face with a genuine skill deficiency. But it still isn't time to assume that a formal training program is needed. By asking a series of questions, you can refine your understanding of why the deficiency exists and shape a solution that gets at the underlying cause.

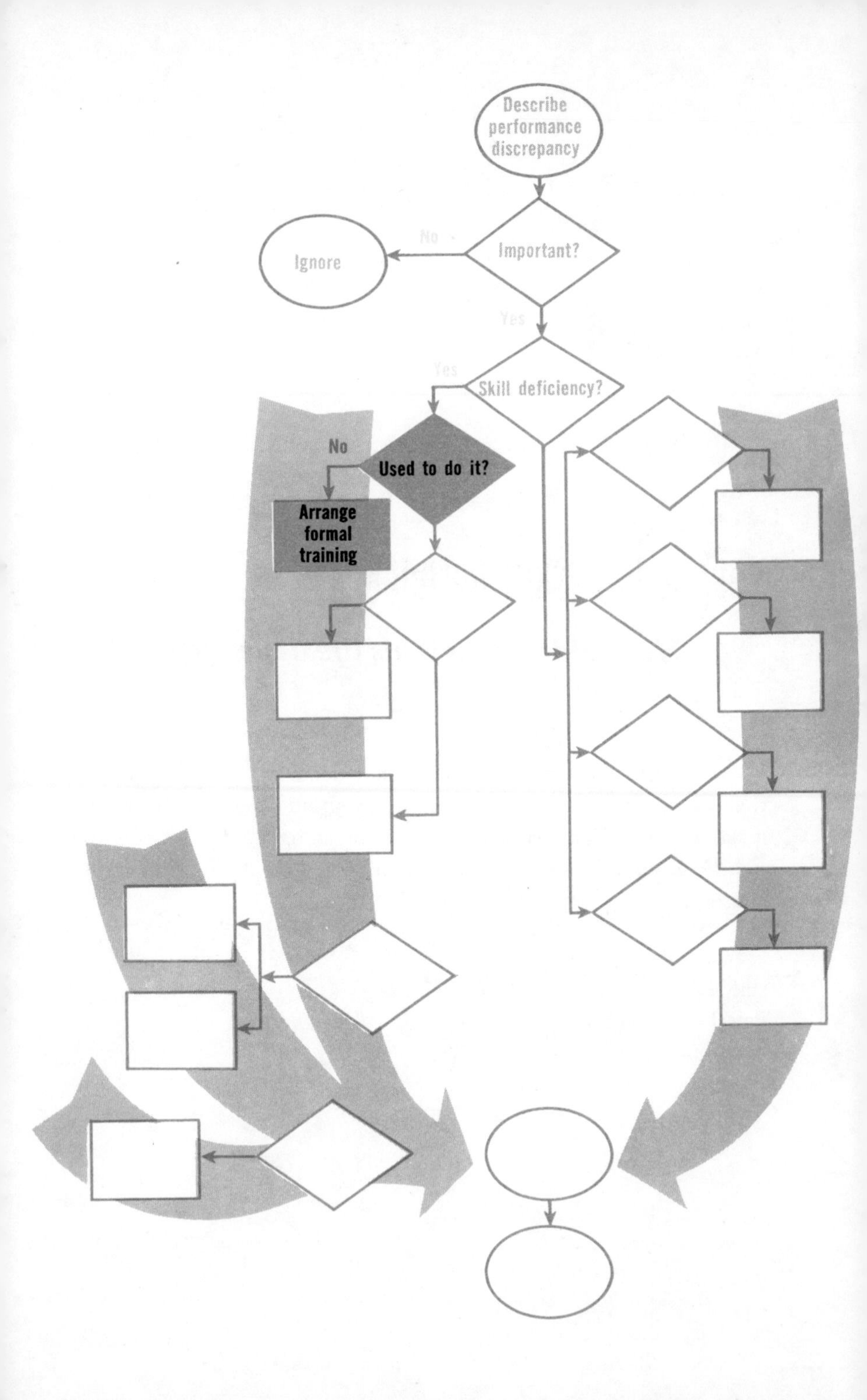

Describe performance discrepancy
Important?
No
Ignore
Yes
Skill deficiency?
Yes
No
Used to do it?
Arrange formal training

CHAPTER 4

Could He Do It in the Past?

■ WHERE WE ARE

A performance discrepancy exists and is considered important. It has been established that it is a genuine skill deficiency.

"Shucks," said the elderly gentleman, "I used to know how to do that pretty good. You just give me a day or two to practice the kinks out and I'll be right in there with the best of 'em."

If he's right, what a waste it would be to start teaching him the skill from the very beginning. In terms of what has to be done to get rid of a skill deficiency, there's a great difference between the skill that *used to be* and the skill that *never was*. Yet the number of instances in which we make the mistake of trying to teach someone something he already knows is very large indeed.

So the thing to do next is ask: Could he do it in the past?

Determining whether a lack of skill is due to a form of forgetting or to a lack of training is one of the more important decisions in the analysis of performance discrepancies. It's also one of the more neglected decisions.

(Even when it's plain that a genuine skill deficiency exists and that our man has *never had* the skill, the solution is not necessarily a formal training program. This issue is explored in Chapter 6, but it isn't too early for a cautionary note: Beware of conclusions about the existence of genuine deficiencies. It's amazing how many courses are given under the assumption that students know nothing whatsoever about the main topic until taught otherwise. All of the students are made to wade through all of the material from the beginning. This can waste a great deal of time, and it may create misconceptions about the effectiveness of a course where the teacher succeeds in "teaching" what the students already knew.)

Anyone who has ever gotten involved with children and ended up cricking his back while playing games or bending his ego in foundering over eighth-grade mathematics will agree that time can play havoc with skills that used to exist. It happens in jobs, too. Consider this example.

Several years ago, one of us was a member of a team assigned to assess the proficiency of radar maintenance men who had graduated from a military course designed to teach that skill. The team traveled to locations around the country to test each maintenance man on his own equipment. While the maintenance man waited outside, the team "inserted a trouble" in his radar equipment. He was then shown one symptom, much as it happens when a radar operator discovers that something isn't working.

One young man tested did an incredibly poor job, even though he had done well during his training. He hardly knew where things were located, let alone what to do to find the trouble. Here, it seemed, was a performance discrepancy of large proportions. When the results of the test were reported, as was required, his commanding officer exploded.

"Get that man in here," he roared. "I'll *teach him* to make our unit look bad."

Fortunately, he was persuaded to sit still for a few questions.

"How long has this man been assigned to your unit?" he was asked.

"About six months."

"What has he been doing during that time?"

"He's been assigned as an oiler."

"How much time has he spent inside the radar van?"

"Well, none. I just told you he's been assigned as an oiler."

"So he hasn't had any practice or experience in radar maintenance since he joined your outfit?"

"... No, I guess not."

Here, then, was a maintenance man who had spent several months learning a rather complex skill; but for six months he had had no opportunity to practice that skill. No wonder his test performance was poor. No wonder there was a difference between what he could do and what he was expected to be able to do.

The battery commander also saw the point. Instead of chastising the maintenance man, he assigned him immediately to maintenance duty (under the watchful eye of a more experienced man).

This was an instance in which:

- There was a genuine performance discrepancy.
- It was important.
- It was due to a skill deficiency.
- The skill was once there, but had been forgotten.

It was a classic case of a skill withering away for lack of exercise. Other examples are not hard to find.

The manager of an engineering group found himself involved with one of those "panic" projects that somehow keep imposing themselves on our routines. His staff had only 36 hours in which to complete preparation of a rather complex proposal, and they were busy making calculations, preparing graphs, and editing copy. The manager had been an engineer once himself, so he took out his slide rule, rolled up his sleeves, and joined his staff at work.

Alas, he made error after error. He just couldn't seem to get things right the first time. And it didn't take him long to see the problem. Though he kept his trusty slide rule in the top drawer of his desk, lack of practice led to some forgetting. Some of his slick slipstick skill had silently slipped away (more rusty than trusty?).

Getting a little personal now . . .

RFM: Peter, didn't you used to live in San Francisco?

PP: Yes.

RFM: Then how come you get lost when you drive there?

PP: Come on, now. I don't *always* get lost. Just most of the time.

RFM: Why?

PP: Well, it all seems so familiar that I don't bother with maps—and then I find I've forgotten some of the streets. I don't get much practice any more. Haven't *you* ever forgotten anything from lack of practice?

RFM: Not very much. Only most of what I learned in school.

PP: Wastrel!

RFM: Wait a minute! I remember from seventh grade biology that the esophagus has a pyloric valve on the end of it.

PP: How nice. What else do you remember?

RFM: Ah-h . . . mmm . . . wel-l-l-l . . .

PP: Do you remember how to fill out your income tax form each year when the times comes?

RFM: Who wants to remember *that*?

PP: But you do it every year.

RFM: I could do it *all* year and not have enough practice to get it right. That's a job that screams for simplification.

PP: Yes. They really oughta wanna simplify that job—instead of trying to make us all into tax experts.

In none of these cases would we propose the expensive route of formal courses of instruction. If we want to sustain these once-known skills at an acceptable level, then the need is probably for a "skill maintenance program" of the kind described in the next chapter.

For now, we will simply call your attention to the importance of those questions that help you decide whether a skill deficiency is due to some form of forgetting or to the fact that it never existed. If it never existed, there's a good chance that training will be indicated. But if it once existed and now is lost, strayed, or stolen, training from scratch would be more of a remedy than you need.

Whether you answer "yes" or "no" to "Could he do it in the past?" (Did he once know how to perform as desired?), you still can't tell what the problem is. More questions are needed. We'll make a start on them in the next chapter.

What to do

Determine whether the skill once existed.

How to do it

Ask these questions:

- Did he once know how to perform as desired?
- Has he forgotten how to do what I want him to do?

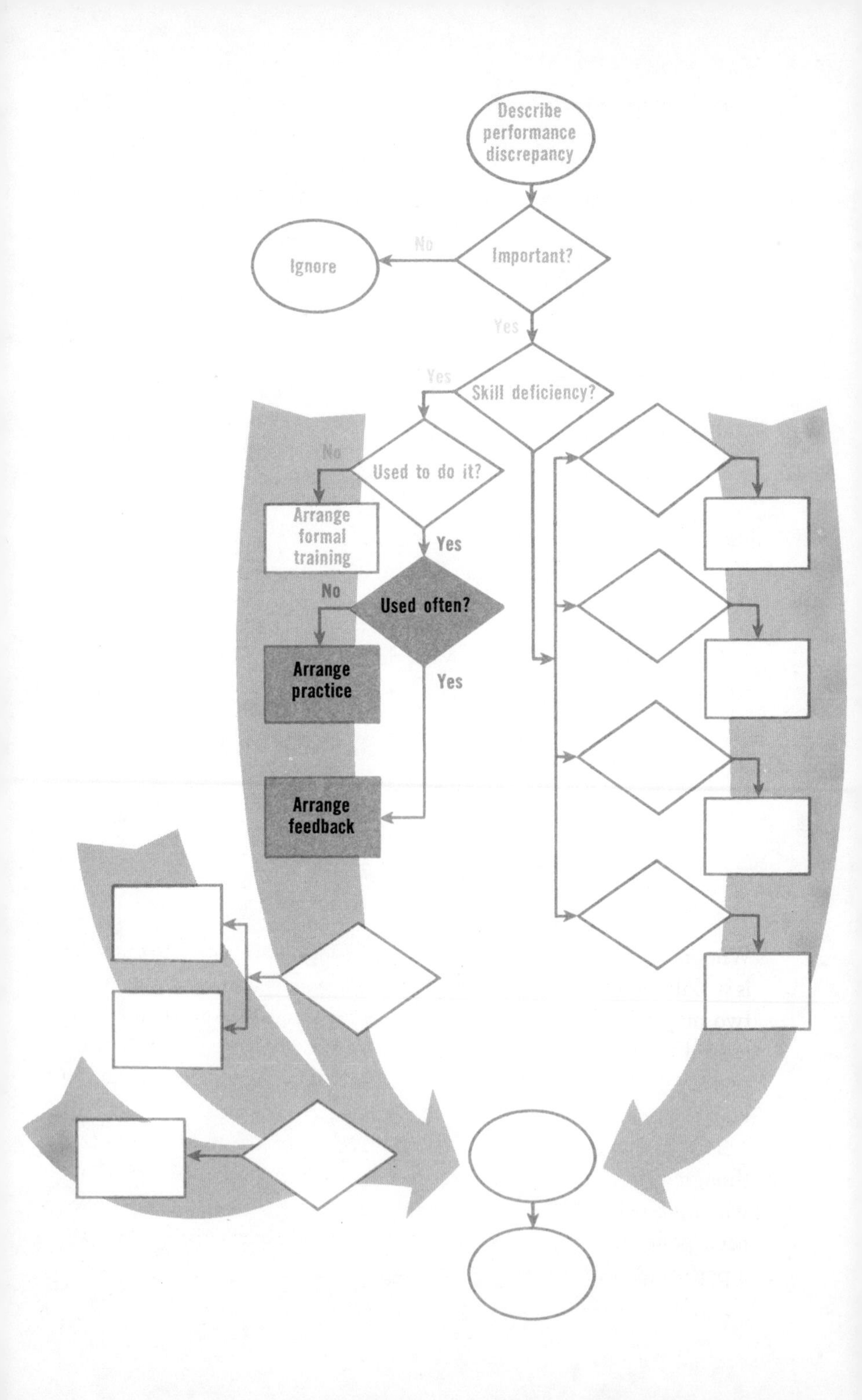
Describe performance discrepancy
Important?
No
Ignore
Yes
Skill deficiency?
Yes
Used to do it?
No
Arrange formal training
Yes
Used often?
No
Arrange practice
Yes
Arrange feedback

CHAPTER 5

Is the Skill Used Often?

■ WHERE WE ARE

An important performance discrepancy exists, and it is a genuine skill deficiency. At one time our man was able to perform as desired.

When a skill fades or disappears, an appropriate remedy to consider is a skill maintenance program. Skill maintenance programs come in two major forms. One kind, as was the case with the radar man discussed in the preceding chapter, is meant to help someone "stay in practice." It is a systematic honing of an important skill or state of knowledge that has to be used only occasionally.

The police departments of the country recognized long ago that though a policeman rarely uses his gun, he must be accurate with it when the need arises. To keep his accuracy within acceptable limits, each policeman is required to practice regularly on a pistol range—a performance maintenance program.

The concert pianist practices and practices between concerts, not only to increase his skill, but to maintain it. He knows that the fine edge of his existing skill can deteriorate rather quickly.

Both of these examples are cases in which performance (and peak performance at that) is required only occasionally or infrequently. In these cases, periodic practice is the useful remedy. The more critical the skill, the more important that this practice be provided.

But there is another type of situation in which the second kind of skill maintenance program is needed, practice with feedback. This is the case where:

- A skill deficiency exists.
- The person used to be able to perform the skill well.
- *The skill is in constant use.*

These are situations in which, paradoxically, performance deteriorates *despite* constant practice. And this is a totally different problem from situations where performance withered away because of lack of practice.

But isn't it true that "practice makes perfect"?

Unfortunately, that ragged old adage is misleading. Practice makes perfect *only* when you have information about how well you are practicing. In fact, if you have no way of knowing how well you are doing, practice may serve merely to entrench poor or imperfect actions. Your marksmanship with a gun will not be improved if you merely shoot at the moon. Your pronunciation of a foreign language will not improve unless you can hear the difference between your way of speaking and a native's way of speaking. Practice without feedback is of little value.

The Case of the Slipping Solderers

In an electronics assembly plant, high precision was demanded of women soldering components together. On joining the company, they were taught to solder; and they were not allowed on the production line until they could consistently make acceptable solder joints. On the job, it was found that the quality of soldered joints tended to fall off after a few weeks, even though the women made hundreds of joints each day. Why?

It was hard to get feedback about the quality of each soldered joint as it was made. You couldn't necessarily tell just by looking. It wasn't practical to make immediate mechanical and electrical tests of each connection. Faulty work in a subassembly may not have been discovered until many joints had been made by many operators. Tracking down the faulty connection and the operator concerned was possible, but costly.

Once again, a performance maintenance program was useful. This time, though, practice was not the primary function. Here it *maintained* skill level by providing the operator with periodic feedback about the quality of her work. All operators were required to renew their certificate of competence every six months. If they checked out, fine; if not, they were given some brief brush-up training. This, it was found, was enough to keep them up to snuff.

The Case of the Diminishing Driver

A friend recently complained, "That's the *third* traffic ticket I've had in a month. I've been driving for ten years and never had a citation—and all of a sudden they start picking on me!"

Hmmm. Wasn't it more likely that his driving skill had slipped somewhat, even though he got plenty of practice? After all, we don't get feedback for every infraction, for every display of poor or dangerous car handling. There is no one there to inform us each time we forget a turn signal, or cut another driver short, or make a turn from the wrong lane, or follow another car too closely. When we *do* get feedback in the form of a traffic citation, we seldom recognize this as an indication of slipshod driving; instead, there is the tendency to point that ever-ready finger—in someone else's direction. (If fingers were as lethal as 45's, we'd *all* be dead by now.)

Any time performance is something other than what is desired and there is reason to believe that the desired performance could be within the person's capabilities, check to see whether he is receiving regular information about the quality of his performance.

So, if he does it regularly, look for lack of feedback as the probable cause; if he doesn't do it regularly, look for lack of practice as a probable cause. Perhaps it would help to see the situation graphically.

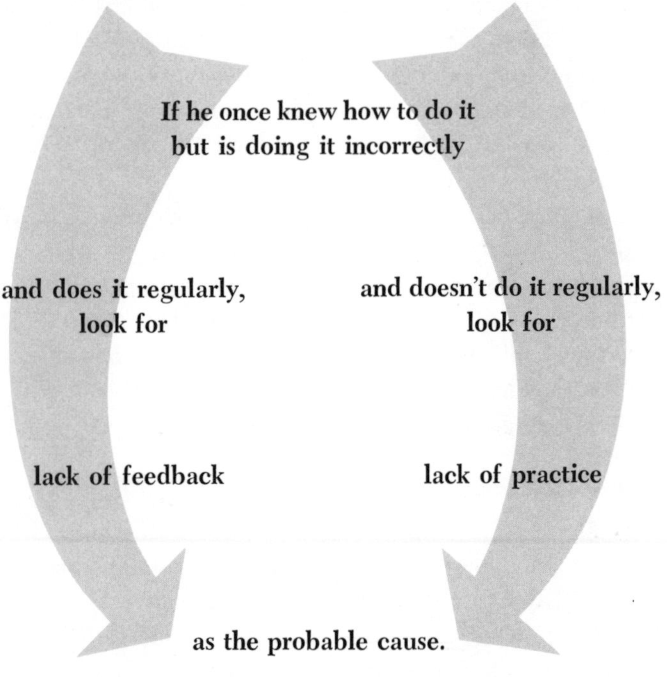

If he once knew how to do it but is doing it incorrectly

and does it regularly, look for

lack of feedback

and doesn't do it regularly, look for

lack of practice

as the probable cause.

As with other causes of performance deficiencies, one of the possible remedies is to change or simplify the job, to modify the performance that is required or expected. As an example, the captain of a big jet, no matter how grizzled and wise he may be, must use a checklist to ensure that he covers everything in his preflight inspection. There's nothing unprofessional about using such an aid; in fact, the unprofessional person is the one who tries to get away without using the checklist. Thus, in addition to, or instead of trying to upgrade someone's performance, even if that performance once existed, you can sometimes solve the problem by providing help. Examples will be offered in Chapter 6.

What to do

Determine whether the lost or deteriorated skill is used frequently or infrequently.

- *If the skill is used frequently* but has deteriorated despite regular use, maintain the level of performance by providing periodic feedback.
- *If the skill is used infrequently*, maintain the level of performance by providing a regular schedule of practice.

How to do it

Ask these questions:

- How often is the skill or performance used?
- Does he get regular feedback about how well he performs?
- Exactly how does he find out how well he is doing?

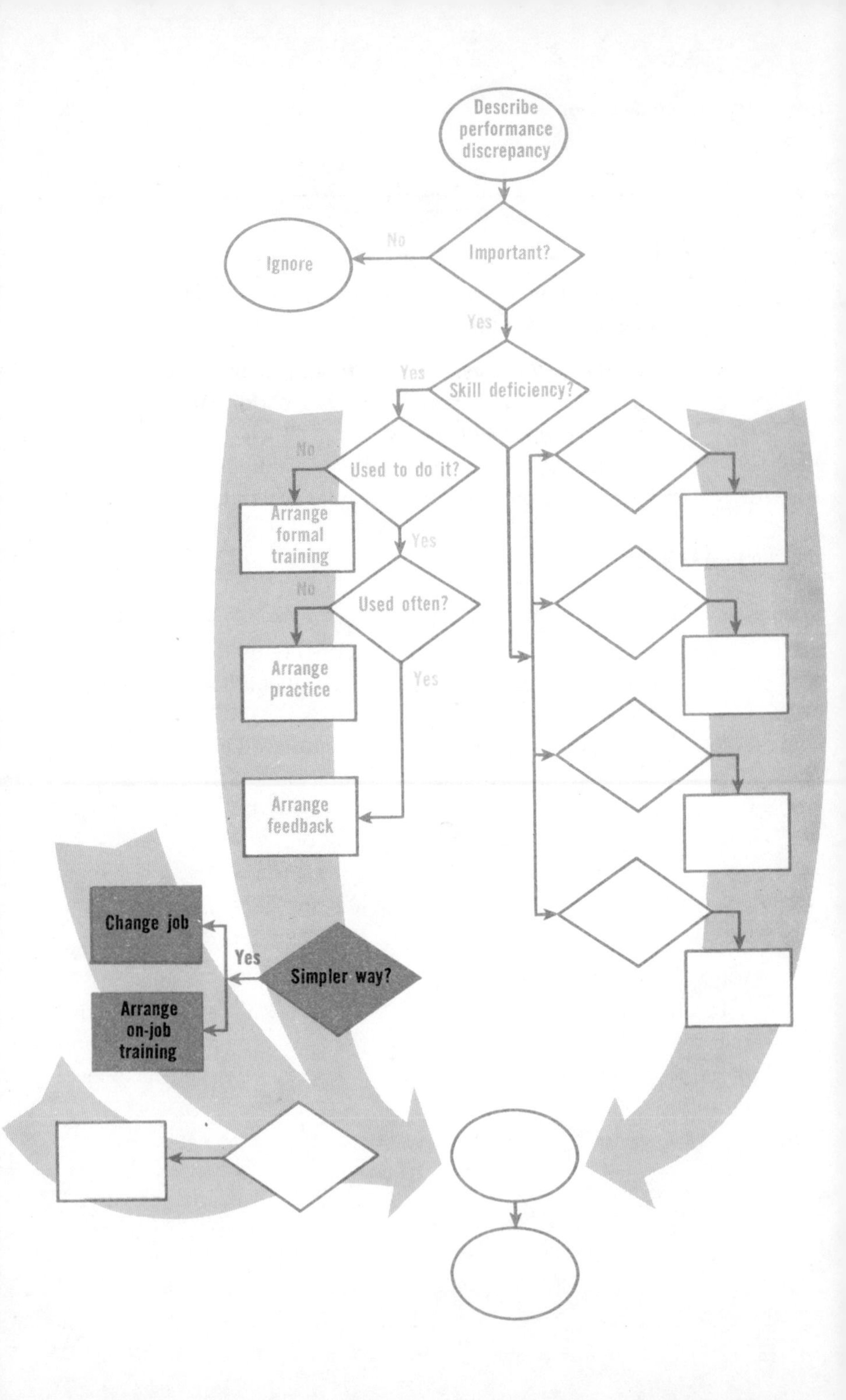
Describe performance discrepancy
Important?
No
Ignore
Yes
Skill deficiency?
Yes
Used to do it?
No
Arrange formal training
Yes
Used often?
No
Arrange practice
Yes
Arrange feedback
Change job
Yes
Simpler way?
Arrange on-job training

CHAPTER 6

Is There a Simpler Solution?

■ WHERE WE ARE

An important performance discrepancy exists. It's a genuine skill deficiency, something he cannot do. Depending upon other conditions, three tentative solutions have been identified: (1) If he used to do it but uses the skill only rarely, consider systematic practice. (2) If he used to do it and still gets lots of practice, consider providing more feedback. (3) If he has never done it, consider formal training.

We are still only exploring possibilities. We have three tentative solutions, but there are two more questions to ask about each situation before the problem can be clearly defined: (1) Is there a simpler way? (2) Does he have the potential to benefit from this solution?

In answer to the first question, there's one universal alternative that may be simpler and less expensive than any solution so far proposed. It's changing the job—changing the skill requirements to meet the skills available. Examples of changing the job:

- If, instead of requiring someone to remember a sequence of steps, you provide him with a checklist to which he can refer any time he wants to know what to do next, you have changed the job. You have simplified it, and presumably it can now be handled by someone with lesser capabilities.

- If you provide machinery for lifting heavy loads, so that an individual no longer has to lift manually, you have changed the job. You have done away with the need for certain physical characteristics. On the other hand, you may have added a need for the ability to master the use of the machinery.

We hope that this sounds obvious. In practice, it may be less obvious. Somehow, tasks themselves, the standards, or the means of performing can become hallowed by precedent ("That's the way it's always been done"), or by apparent acceptance in high places ("That's how the boss wants it done"), or through many other appeals to authenticity that make the present desired performance the one and only way.

Examples are all around us of ways in which a task has been simplified through the use of instructions, aids, or checklists, eliminating the need for formal instruction. Any number of household appliances, for example, require that you learn something before they can be used properly. But their manufacturers don't provide a course; they provide a leaflet or booklet. And a look at the instructions is generally enough to do the trick.

A rather similar solution works well when the knowledge needed to carry out an infrequent task is simple to acquire. Rather than teach a course, and try to store information in the head of every potential user, you put instructions where they can be readily seen. For example, if you have forgotten how to use a fire extinguisher, instructions carried on the device will refresh your memory in a second or two. Bought a new car? Read the manual and you will be ready to go; no course needed.

In the best of all possible worlds, every household might have available at all times a person able to render first aid for all conceivable cases of poisoning. But most of us take care of that problem adequately enough by fastening a list of poison antidotes to the door of the broom closet The specifics of what to do in each particular situation are, in fact, better stored on the closet door than in someone's head. A wait of a minute or two might be less dangerous than giving the victim the wrong antidote.

The situation is similar for the "critical" skill known as fire drill. We have people practice fire drill procedures so that they will be able to get out of a burning building by the quickest and safest route. We may also institute emergency procedures, such as telephoning for help. But we also display the emergency telephone number by the bedside, and we attach instructions for using the fire extinguisher to the extinguisher itself.

You can just imagine the chaos if every person who prepared airline tickets had to *remember* all the information there is to know about flight times, destinations, flight numbers, days the flights are operative, and a gaggle of other details. Even if such were possible, the problem would be multiplied every time there was a *change* in the schedule. With the information stuffed into a manual or a computer instead of into someone's head, it is easily and accurately available and easy to change.

The more complex the job, or the more critical it is that it be performed correctly, the stronger the argument for introducing a performance aid rather than expecting people to be "fully trained." If you have a task that is performed infrequently and which is also both complex and critical, you have every reason to find ways of reducing the need for such human skills as recall and judgment.

Industry has found that errors can be eliminated by labeling the controls of equipment. Color coding can also reduce errors and the need for training. Color coded pathways on warehouse floors tell forklift operators where to travel and where to store what; color coded gas tanks tell the anesthesiologist their content; gas pumps at the service station are color coded for easier recognition; price tags in the dress shop are often color coded according to dress size; and sets of books are often color coded by a publisher for easier identification.

Consider the case of the meter readers. Women at the end of a production line making electronic products recorded the electrical characteristics of each product so that an accept/reject decision could be made. To do so, they took about six readings from as many meters, and wrote down the numbers on a card.

In an ordinary day, each woman made hundreds of readings; and many of them had had months, even years, of experience. But when their meter reading accuracy was measured one day, it was found to be only 40 percent! Interestingly, a group of housewives with no special training in reading meters performed at the same level.

How could this be? If experience is the best teacher, why didn't the meter readers get better rather than worse?

The answer proved to be that they never found out whether their readings were accurate. In time, their accuracy diminished.

Aha! Isn't the answer obvious? Where there is no feedback for performance, the thing to do is to arrange for feedback. Sometimes, though, that's easier said than done, as in this case. So what's the alternative? Nearly always, one possibility is to change the job so as to eliminate the performance for which it is difficult to arrange feedback. Here, the company provided an aid to performance by installing meters that show their reading directly in numerals rather than by the movement of a pointer along a scale.

If you've reached this point via the argument that leads to "consider formal training," you have special reason to be wary, since formal training is probably the most expensive solution of all. It pays to take an extra-hard second look when your instinctive response is "We need another course."

A few years ago, the powers-that-be asked the instructional technology department of a British military group to determine if some programmed instruction would be useful in a five-day course in the maintenance of teletypewriter equipment. The course had been continually refined throughout its existence, but the management wanted to make it even better. The instructional technologists knew their trade, however, and didn't fall into the trap of just looking at the existing curriculum to see what pieces of it might be programmed. Instead, they performed a task analysis to see what the repairman did when performing his job. They started from the beginning in order to find out whether there was a discrepancy between what students *entering* the course could do and what they were required to do on the job. They wanted to know if that discrepancy was a genuine skill deficiency.

It was, and so they asked questions to determine how best to eliminate the discrepancy. As a result, not only did they *not* prepare any programmed instruction for the existing course, but the existing course was, as they say in England, disestablished. Cancelled.

Why? Because they found that what trainees needed to learn could easily be picked up on the job with observation and informal instruction and practice. Formal instruction was a more elaborate solution than needed, like using an elephant to crack peanuts or a computer to add the grocery bill. Had the analysis been conducted before the course was set up in the first place, it is doubtful that such an extensive effort would have been proposed to stuff into the students' heads that which was either not needed or already there.

In summary, even when a genuine skill deficiency exists, any solution to the problem should be weighed against the possibility of changing the job, particularly through providing some kind of job aid–checklists, instruction sheets, signs, labels, color coding, etc. If training seems to be the only remedy, on-the-job training may be easier and cheaper and just as good as the formal variety. As one of the sages of the business, Thomas Gilbert, puts it, "Show-how is cheaper than know-how."

What to do

Determine if there is a solution simpler than performance maintenance or formal training.

How to do it

Ask these questions:

- Can I change the job by providing some kind of job aid?
- Can I store the needed information some way (written instructions, checklists) other than in someone's head?
- Can I show rather than train?
- Would informal (on-the-job) training be sufficient?

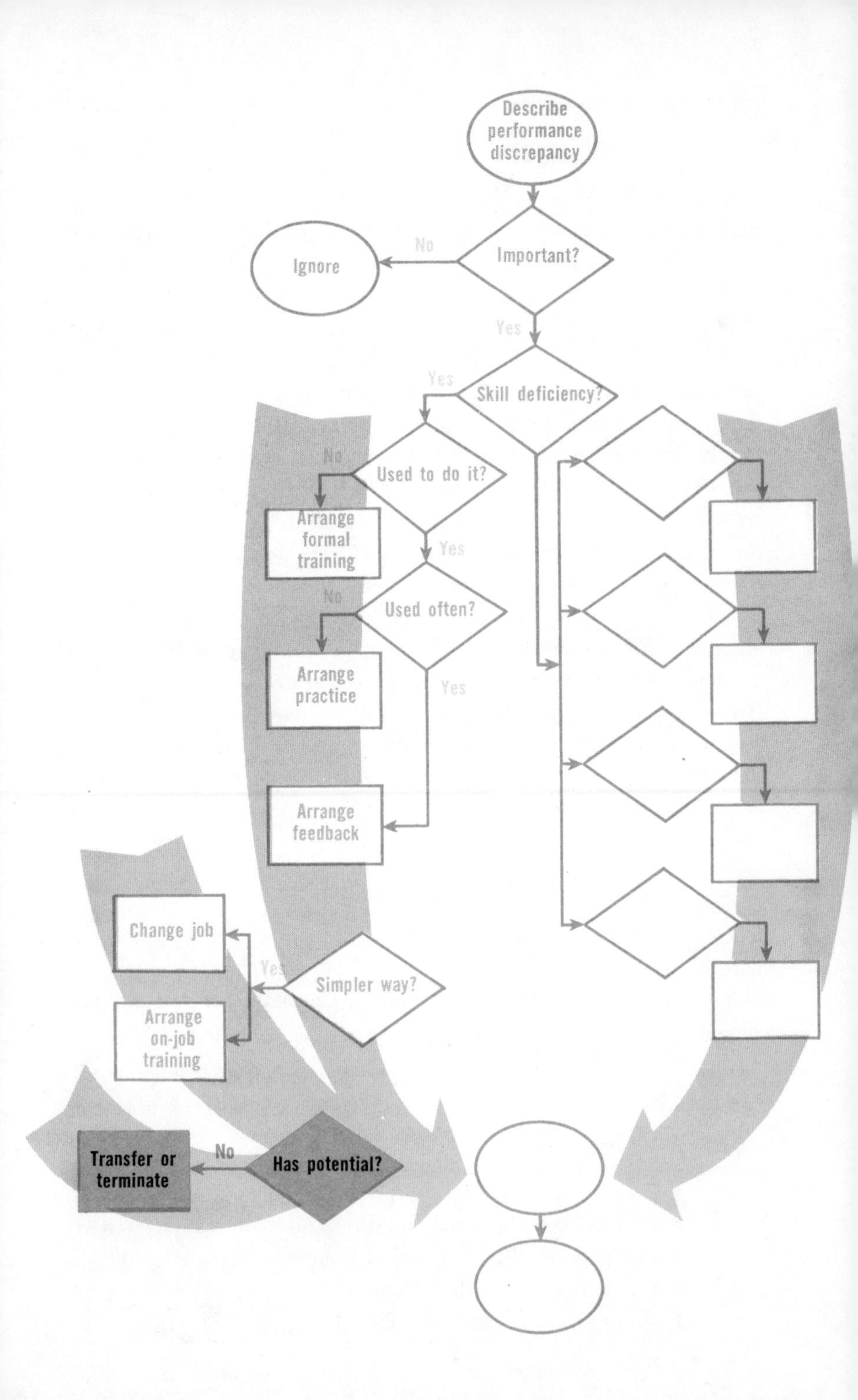
Describe performance discrepancy
Important?
No
Ignore
Yes
Skill deficiency?
Yes
Used to do it?
No
Arrange formal training
Yes
Used often?
No
Arrange practice
Yes
Arrange feedback
Change job
Yes
Simpler way?
Arrange on-job training
Transfer or terminate
No
Has potential?

CHAPTER 7

Does He Have What It Takes?

■ WHERE WE ARE

An important performance discrepancy has been identified as a genuine skill deficiency. Depending upon conditions, we have identified one of the following as a possible solution: (1) Provide feedback to keep a frequently-used skill up to standard, or *(2) provide periodic practice to sustain an infrequently-used skill,* or *(3) provide formal training,* or *(4) provide some simpler type of training,* or *(5) change the requirements of the job.*

All five of our possible ways of tackling different causes of genuine deficiencies in performance must still be considered tentative. One more dimension must be added to our statement of the problem by asking this question: Does he have the potential to benefit from this change?

You can make all the changes you like, but if your man doesn't have what it takes to do the job, either mentally or physically, the changes are a waste of time.

Any time someone cannot handle an existing job, you're stuck, inevitably, with the two universal alternatives to all of the solutions proposed in this book: change the job or change the man. The first alternative was discussed in the previous chapter. The second is the subject of this chapter.

"Changing the man" means, of course, to substitute another person for the apparent nonperformer. Sometimes it's quite plain that this is inevitable, as when physical limitations prevent performance. The decision to transfer or fire is not always as straightforward as it may seem when your patience is running out, however. In fact, to look at a problem with anger or impatience is to look at it through a distorting lens.

On a production line making very tiny products, for example, a foreman complained that one girl made considerably more mistakes than anyone else. Like the others, she peered through a binocular microscope to see the tiny parts and to assist with their assembly. She assembled the same product as the others, and under the same conditions. But she was considerably "clumsier" than the others. The foreman wanted to get rid of her; that was his solution.

This case came to the attention of the training department, and its members looked around and asked questions. They quickly discovered that this girl was not looking through the microscope with *both* eyes as she should have been. She looked with only one eye at a time. She didn't know that looking with both eyes at the same time made any difference when the instrument was properly adjusted. But without the depth perception that comes with using both eyes simultaneously, she could not see well enough to assemble accurately. Hence, she was labeled "clumsy."

After only two or three *minutes* instruction in the proper use of the microscope, this girl's work was the equal of all the others in the department. She wasn't clumsy, or unmotivated, or incapable of learning. She was simply prevented from doing the job well by lack of information.

The remedies of transfer and termination are used more often than they should be. They are the crude hatchets of those unsophisticated in their knowledge of the limits of human performance, a sign of failure to locate less traumatic remedies. They should be considered a last resort rather than a first.

The issue of "potential to perform" should be approached in two stages: Could he learn the job? Does he have what it takes to do the job?

If he can learn it he can do it, can't he? Not necessarily. It sounds contradictory, but some people become under-performers because they are over-qualified for what they are doing.

Some companies court trouble without realizing it by following a policy of over-hiring. "We always hire the best people available," they boast; and then they go on to set people to work at jobs that are beneath their abilities. College graduates are put to work as glorified typists, or given simple tasks on a production line; engineers find themselves working in the drafting department. Managers who succumb to this temptation are bewildered when dissatisfaction appears in its many guises—low morale, absenteeism, edginess, uncooperativeness, and so on.

In a company we know, inspectors tested some complex electronic devices at the end of assembly. They did so by connecting the devices to their test equipment and checking readings on dials. The day shift inspector was a motherly type who had little idea of *why* she was doing these things. She simply hooked up the devices and recorded the readings. If the readings deviated from those specified, she rejected the device.

The night shift inspection, on the other hand, was handled by a young woman who was a doctoral candidate in the arts at a nearby university. She found an intellectual challenge in any task. Rather than sit around and grow bored, she worked hard at finding out all she could about the how and why of the manufacture of the devices. Eventually, she was able to hold an intelligent conversation about the devices with engineers. Because of her increased knowledge, she began to *interpret* the readings on her test equipment. She no longer adhered to the strict accept/reject instructions. As a result, she began to accept devices that should not have been accepted, and to send others back for expensive reworking when they should have been accepted.

It's always a temptation to put the "best" available person into a job. But when he's much over-qualified, the rewards can be short-lived. A more realistic matching of skills with jobs will avoid the boredom and lack of challenge that lead to performance discrepancies after the first rush of enthusiasm.

The problem of over-qualification can arise at home, too. Take the case of the teen-ager assigned to the carrying-out-the-garbage detail. The young are notoriously (and perhaps rightly) impatient of activities they consider boring. So the teen-ager fights carrying out the garbage. ("I'm his father/mother," you say. "Why should I get stuck with this chore when I have this great lummox on hand? Isn't it boring for me, too?" Yes, of course. But, emotional issues aside, the teen-ager is bored and wants to be involved in something more exciting. Garbage-carrying loses out when it competes with doing, or even dreaming about, most other activities. The rewards of garbage-carrying have to be competitive with those real or imagined delights —a good trick. The least this tells you is that those who work at tasks for which they are over-qualified need some extrinsic reward to take the place of "satisfaction in the job." More on that later.)

In summary, it is useful to determine whether someone has the capacity to do the job required, and whether he would "fit" the job mentally and motivationally even if his performance were brought up to standard. If the answer to both questions is "yes," go ahead with your solution.

What to do

Determine whether the person has the potential to perform as desired.

How to do it

Ask these questions:

- Could he learn the job?
- Does he have the physical and mental potential to perform as desired?
- Is he over-qualified for the job?

PART III

It Is Not a Skill Deficiency.

He could do it if he wanted to.

Could he do it if he had to? This pivotal question was asked immediately after we determined that we were looking at an important performance discrepancy (Chapter 3). To this point, we've looked at several solutions that apply when the answer is plainly "No. Even if we held a gun at his head, he couldn't do it." Now we're going back to the question to see what happens when the answer is something other than that unequivocal "no."

When you know or suspect that a person could perform if he really had to, it's probably plain that something other than instruction is needed. In general, the remedy is that of *performance management*. Rather than modify the person's skill or knowledge (since it's likely that he already has the ability), you will have to modify the conditions associated with the performance, or the consequence or result of that performance. Rather than change what he *can* do, change something about the world in which he does it so that doing it will be more attractive, or less repulsive, or less difficult.

You will get clues that a problem is mainly one of performance management rather than performance teaching from statements such as:

"He just isn't motivated."
"He just doesn't *want* to do it."
"He simply doesn't *care*."
"He's too lazy to do it."
"He doesn't have the right attitude."
"He oughta wanna do it."
"I'm too busy to do it."
"I'm not allowed to do it."
"That isn't my job."
"They'll fire me if I do it."
"They'll laugh at me if I do it."
"Not now, honey . . . later."

These statements hint that the person probably *could* perform as desired, but isn't. They suggest that the skill in question is already within the repertoire of the person being described, but that it is not being used. They are the clues that indicate a situation that might be described as "plenty of skill but not enough will." You can be pretty sure that to influence him to do it you must change the environment around the performance in some way rather than try to add to his skills.

There are four general causes of such nonperformance:

1. It is punishing to perform as desired.
2. It is rewarding to perform other than as desired.
3. It simply doesn't matter whether performance is as desired.
4. There are obstacles to performing as desired.

We will consider what each of these causes looks like in real life, and offer key questions for spotting them. We'll also suggest remedies.

Once again, we emphasize that no sequence of priority or importance is implied by the order in which we have listed the causes or the position in which we have placed them in the flow diagram.

Consider them in any order you prefer. We urge only that you consider all of them before deciding that your analysis is complete. Usually, it will pay you to go over them more than once, since each answer you get may change your perception of the problem.

We now return to the point in our flow diagram where we determined whether the discrepancy in performance was due to a skill deficiency. This time we will look at the implications of "No. This is *not* a case of skill deficiency."

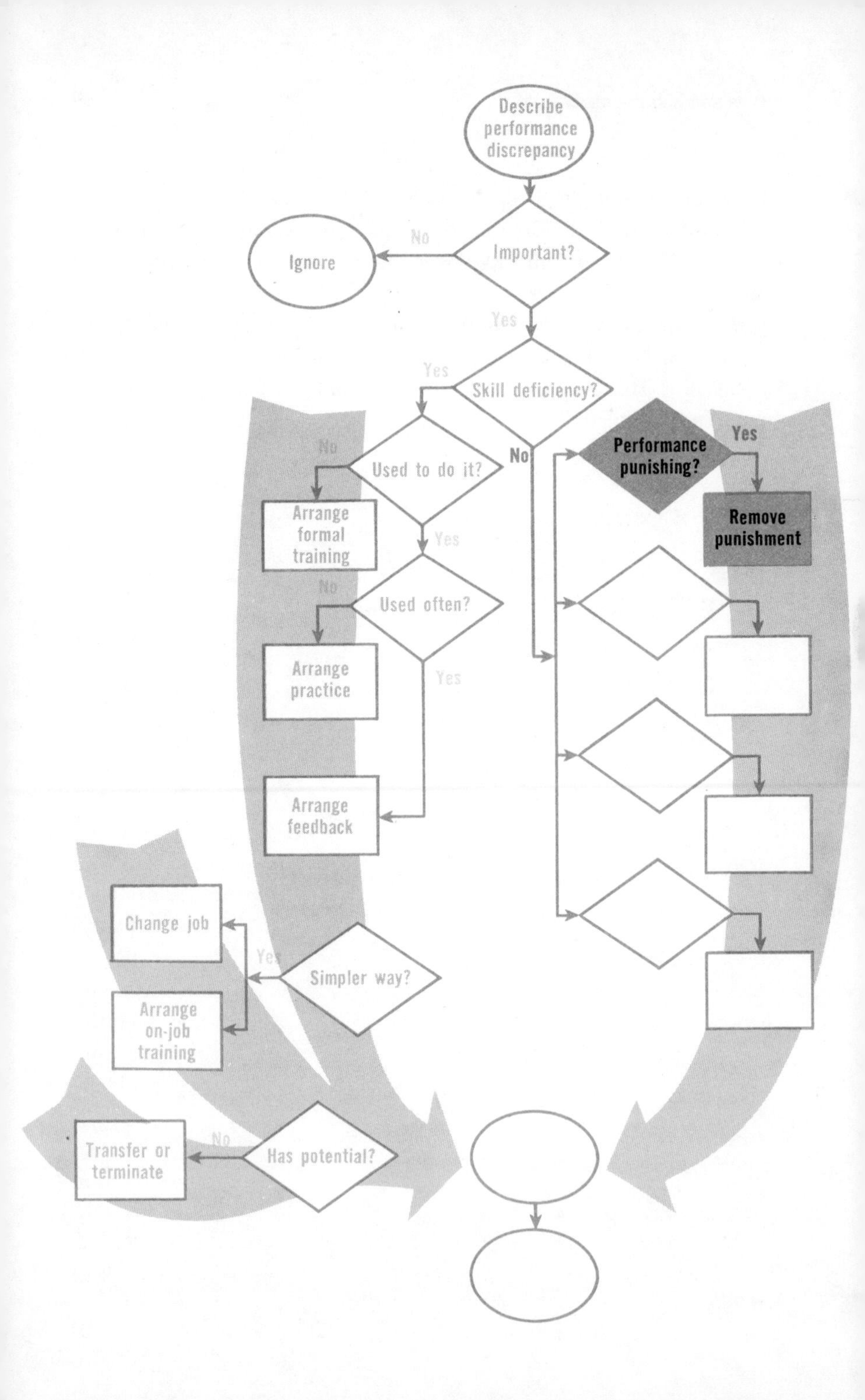
Describe performance discrepancy
No
Important?
Ignore
Yes
Skill deficiency?
Yes
No
Used to do it?
No
Yes
Arrange formal training
Used often?
No
Yes
Arrange practice
Arrange feedback
Performance punishing?
Yes
Remove punishment
Change job
Yes
Simpler way?
Arrange on-job training
Transfer or terminate
No
Has potential?

CHAPTER 8

Is Desired Performance Punishing?

■ WHERE WE ARE

An important discrepancy is known or suspected not *to be due to a skill deficiency. (That is, he could do it if he had to or if he wanted to.)*

One reason people don't do as they are expected to do is simply that the desired "doing" is punishing. And when desired performance leads to undesirable results, people have a way of finding other ways to go. Here are several examples.

A college music student had the chance to play with his city's symphony orchestra. For a student who had not yet completed his training, this was a rare opportunity. Since he needed both the money and the experience, he asked his music teacher if something could be worked out.

"I think so," replied the teacher. "There is no reason why you shouldn't take the job, provided you make up the school work you miss on the days you are absent."

So, the student threw himself into both tasks. He did well with the symphony and earned "A's" and "B's" on all his make-up work. But when grading time arrived, he found himself with a "C" for the course. Astonished, he asked his teacher why he was given only a "C" after receiving "A's" and "B's" for all his work.

She replied: "Well, you're getting entirely too much experience and not enough learning."

If you were the student, how would you feel in such a situation? No matter how you slice it, this is a situation in which desirable activity is followed by an unpleasant consequence (punishment). If, as a result of this dampening, the student were to perform his school work with less enthusiasm, one can imagine the teacher telling her colleagues, "You know, we've got to teach him to have the right attitude about his studies. He oughta wanna have more interest."

Punishment for desired or superior performance is so common that one may overlook it in an area where it frequently occurs—the family. Yet it's plain to see in neighborhoods where the norm is anti-intellectual. Sons or daughters who aspire to rise above the intellectual level of their relatives, or who set their sights on occupations different from those pursued by relatives, or who raise their conversations above the level of trivia, are clawed back into the quagmire of mediocrity. They are not applauded, or revered, or urged to greater heights, but instead are insulted and stung with ridicule so that they will not escape their mental ghettos.

There are many more cases around the home where desired performance is withheld because of its unfavorable consequence. Parents complain, "I don't know what they teach 'em in school these days, but our kids don't come to us with their questions and problems like they used to." Observe these same parents in interaction with their children, however, and it quickly becomes apparent that the parents are the cause of the problem.

Kid: Hey, Mom'n Dad! Look what I made in school today!
Parent: Wipe your mouth!

or

Kid: Look at the picture I drew for you, Mom.
Mom: Don't you ever clean your fingernails?

Little wonder the kids behave as they do. The parents, all unintentionally, perhaps, have engineered it that way. And usually they couldn't have done a better job if they had been trying.

These examples are designed to remind you of a simple truth about human behavior:

People learn to avoid the things they are hit with!

It doesn't matter whether they are hit with a club, an insult, humiliation, repeated failure, frustration, or boredom. If someone feels he will be punished, or even that there is a risk of being punished when he performs as you desire, he will avoid doing it your way whenever he can. People don't often do things that will lead to their world being dimmer than it is.

And so, when someone isn't performing as desired, and you know that he *could* do so, one thing to explore is whether it isn't unnecessarily punishing to perform that way. Is there an undesirable consequence (result) for doing it your way? Does he see desired performance as being geared to penalties? If so, you have probably located a strong reason why you aren't getting the results you would like.

We must emphasize, however, that it is not *your* view of the outcome that is important here. You must try to see the situation through the eyes of the person whose performance you would change and ask yourself, "What is the result to *him* for doing as I desire? How might *he* see the consequence of doing it?" What may be a favorable consequence to *you* may be *un*favorable to *him*.

On occasion, this can be subtle. Sometimes it may strike you as ridiculous. No matter. Listen to what the performer says.

The employer says, "I don't see why he won't work overtime—he makes good money on it." But the employee says, "What's the good of overtime. Anything you earn, they take away in taxes."

The parent says, "I don't see why he won't take math. It will get him a better job when he's grown." But the student says, "Math is for the guys who want to follow the establishment road. I'm interested in people. Besides, the math teacher is the least liked guy in the whole school."

Or consider the case of the "rate buster" in school or industry—the one who turns out more work than anyone else. Is he revered by his colleagues for his skill or his industriousness? It's likely that he will soon perceive the group's attitude toward him as punishment for performance, and he'll slow down to the level of the group . . . or be pushed out of it.

Did you ever attend a school where the consequence of knowing your subject or of showing your intelligence was ridicule from other students, where the "in" thing was not to do homework and not to make good grades, where diligent students were dismissed as "eggheads" and "brains" and worse?

You hear teachers and administrators complain that students don't do their homework. "These students oughta wanna do their homework. If they don't, they will be doomed to a lifetime of mediocrity." And then, because teachers and administrators fail to look at the problem from the students' viewpoint, they make new policies that only aggravate the situation.

In such a case, homework is doubly punishing for the student. He perceives it first as an onerous duty that replaces more pleasant activities. If, despite this, he does the homework, it may lead to consequences in which the lumps he takes from his peers may outweigh more positive outcomes such as good grades and teacher approval. So he doesn't do his homework. So the school invents new punitive policies, and more threat of failure is laid on. And so the student perceives yet another reason why it's necessary to beat the system. One can't help thinking of two gladiators beating each other to death with bloodied clubs, each telling the other he oughta wanna be the first to stop. For no matter what the school does, it cannot invent a consequence aversive enough to outweigh the ridicule of peers.

A more effective way to break the miserable chain of events would be to make the consequence of studying more immediately favorable than those that now exist, so that those who study successfully will have reason to be envied rather than ridiculed. Rather than continue to argue that the student "oughta wanna" *for his own good*, make desired privileges dependent upon the performance wanted. Instead of saying, "You will fail if you don't learn," make the rule say that if the student learns he may have an extra free period, or that he will be allowed to come and go as he pleases, or that he will be entitled to some other thing he really finds desirable.

Several years ago the clinical faculty of a dental school complained that students were putting in too little laboratory time on dentures they were making for their patients. The situation was this. Students treated their patients in the clinic. When adjustments were needed in the fitting of dentures, the student would go to the laboratory to make adjustments and then return to the patient in the clinic to try again. The complaint of the faculty was that the students were not as painstaking as they should have been and as they *knew how to be* in getting dentures to fit. "We've got to teach them to be less careless," was the cry. "We've got to teach them to have the right attitude."

So here's another situation in which a person has the skill to perform as desired but for some reason is *not* performing as desired. But what would the faculty "teach" the students to remedy this performance discrepancy? What would they put in a curriculum—molar appreciation? How could they "encourage the right attitude"?

When the question was finally asked, "What is the consequence of performing correctly?" the nature of the problem became obvious. The laboratory was one floor up and at the other end of the building from the clinic. Obviously, it was less punishing to cut a few corners than to run up and down every few minutes. When the lab was finally moved next to the clinic, the quality of the dentures improved miraculously—without any instruction at all.

The hospital provides us with another example of how it is possible to design *against* the results one wants. Patients who cannot get out of bed are provided with a call button with which to summon help. Most of the time, the system works quite well. Occasionally, however, a patient will resist pressing the call button for long periods of time—even though in great distress.

Why doesn't the patient press the button when he is in need? What consequence of pressing the button when he needs help might cause him to suffer? Is it possible button-pushing can somehow be punishing?

You bet it can! It can be embarrassing or upsetting. Occasionally, the consequence of pushing the button is to summon a grouch who bursts into the room with a "What now?" or a "Not *you* again?" It takes few such experiences for the weakened patient to find it easier to tolerate his distress than to press the button for help.

Industry is no less susceptible to the situation in which desired performance is more punishing than need be. For example, the flaunting of safety regulations despite "safety training" is a familiar problem. Though people often know how to recognize and report a safety hazard, they don't. Why not?

In some departments it is considered "rocking the boat" to report safety hazards (it usually implies that someone has been sloppy or irresponsible), and in some others it is considered unmanly ("Only sissies wear goggles," or "You gotta be a l'il ol' lady to use a saw guard.") But regardless of the reason, the consequence of hazard-reporting is punishment. A man may be looked down on by his peers, or he may have to bear the brunt of insults. He may even find the "rules" of the department "explained" to him with a fist. There are places where it simply isn't safe to report safety hazards!

Once a problem of this kind is identified as an example of "performance is punishing," it's plain that the solution is not the usual one of handing out more information. Though there may be a number of actions used as remedies, depending on the precise circumstances, each will have to be a way of reducing the undesirable results and increasing the desirable results of desired performance. Some companies provide a bonus or recognition to departments with perfect safety records, while others may tie desired privileges to an absence of accidents over an extended period of time.

For another common if less important example, take meeting-attending behavior. Time is wasted waiting for latecomers. It persists no matter how often instructions are given or exhortations are delivered. Plainly, this isn't a miniature training problem. To get at the true problem, you have to ask: "What's the consequence of performing as desired?"

What are the results of coming on time? Well, you have to sit around and wait for latecomers.

What's the result of being late? The meeting starts almost as soon as you arrive.

Thus, punctuality is punished and tardiness is rewarded. And that's precisely the opposite of what is intended.

Another interesting problem of this sort came to our attention not long ago. A bank decided, "We've got to teach our branch managers to be a little less conservative about making loans." The remainder of the conversation with management went like this:

"Do these branch managers know how to be riskier about making loans?"

"Yes. They merely have to accept those loan applications closest to the top of the reject pile."

"Do they know you want them to be less conservative?"

"Oh, yes. We have been sending them corporate memos for the past six months, but it doesn't seem to do much good."

"What happens to the branch manager who takes a conservative stance?"

"All his loans are paid back and he is looked at favorably."

"What happens if he takes the riskier stance, as desired?"

"Well, if some of his loans default, his superiors rate his performance down."

As we said, people learn to avoid the things they are hit with.

In summary, when it appears that someone knows how to perform as desired but doesn't, find out whether the desired performance leads to unpleasant results (unpleasant from *his* point of view). If so, the remedy is to find ways to reduce or eliminate the negative effects and to create, or increase the strength of, positive or desirable consequences. (It is quite possible, of course, to offer an incentive for something that someone cannot be expected to do. Such unreasonable expectations can lead not only to frustration on the part of the person trying to perform, but to a feeling of failure—of being no good, of being "bad." Though a favorable consequence will increase the likelihood that desired actions *will* occur, or increase the frequency with which they do occur, it will only do so if the *desired* performance is *possible* performance. As the old saw says, "You can't make a silk purse out of a sow's ear unless you start with a silk sow.")

What to do

Determine whether desired performance leads to unfavorable consequences.

How to do it

Ask these questions:

- What *is* the consequence of performing as desired?
- Is it punishing to perform as expected?
- Does *he* perceive desired performance as being geared to penalties?
- Would his world become a little dimmer (to him) if he performed as desired?

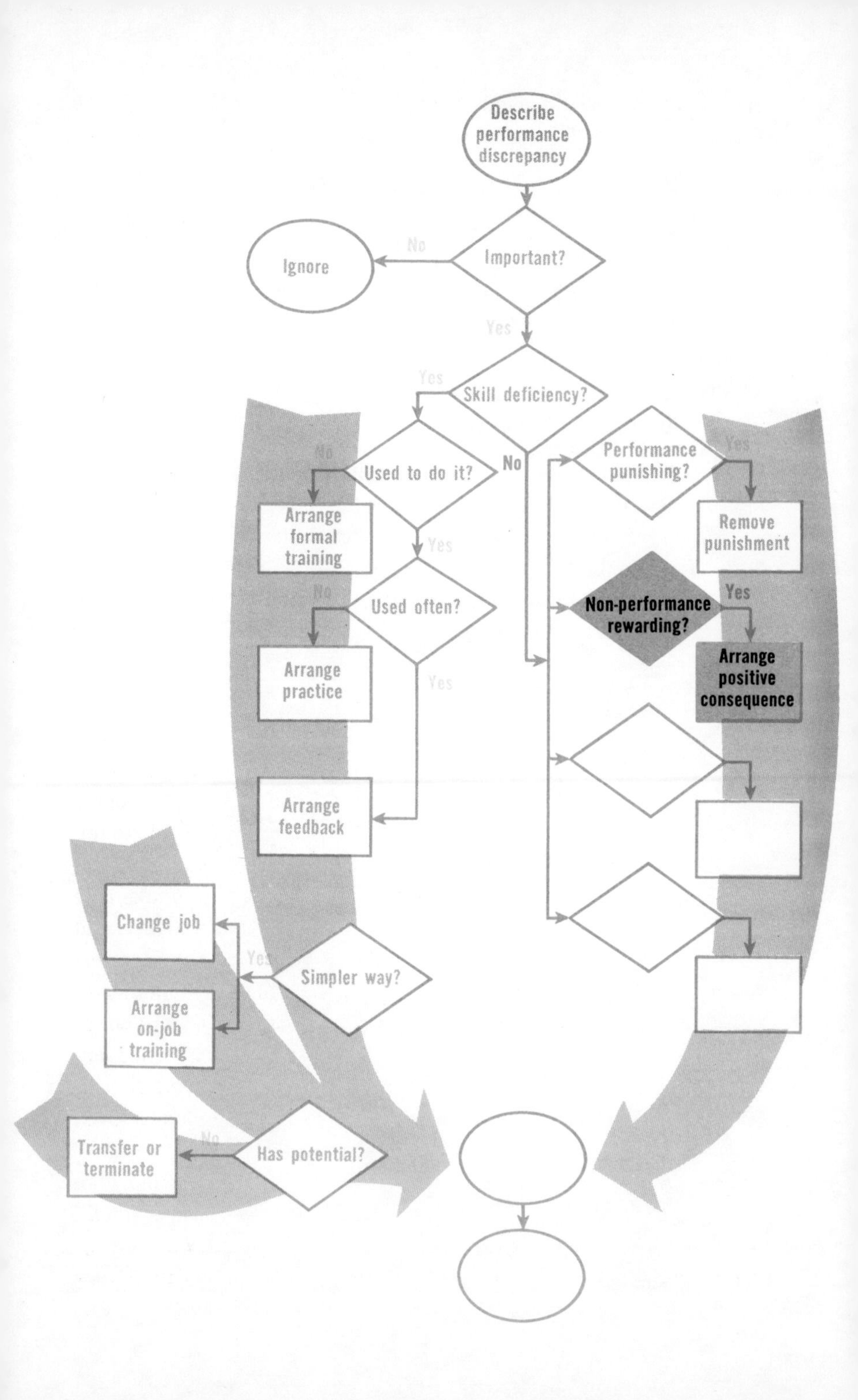

Describe performance discrepancy
Important?
No
Ignore
Yes
Skill deficiency?
Yes
No
Used to do it?
No
Arrange formal training
Yes
Used often?
No
Arrange practice
Yes
Arrange feedback
Performance punishing?
Yes
Remove punishment
Non-performance rewarding?
Yes
Arrange positive consequence
Change job
Yes
Simpler way?
Arrange on-job training
Transfer or terminate
No
Has potential?

CHAPTER 9

Is Non-performance Rewarding?

■ WHERE WE ARE

An important discrepancy is known or suspected not *to be due to a skill deficiency.*

In the last chapter, we examined the fact that sometimes people don't do what they know how to do because the doing leads to unpleasant results. So, in analyzing a performance discrepancy that does not appear to be due to a skill deficiency, one step to take is to see if unpleasant consequences follow the desired performance. But there is another side to that issue. Performance may not be as expected because *non*-performing is *rewarding*. That is, whether or not desired performance has favorable consequences, they are not as favorable as those of an other-than-desired performance. Thus, another step to take when looking for the cause of a "he-could-do-it-if-he-wanted-to-but-he-doesn't-and-he-oughta-wanna" problem is to explore the consequences of the thing he is doing *now*.

Two examples of people performing in ways that are other than desirable include the maternity ward receptionist who makes you fill out a dozen documents when it's obvious that the arrival of your child is imminent, and the petty bureaucrat who counters all of your attempts to get something done with a regulation that says you can't, but who never offers a hint of the right course to follow.

If you take the view that these people are supposed to facilitate rather than obstruct, you have to assume that they are performing in an undesirable manner. Obstructive behavior must be more rewarding than facilitating behavior, even though the formal rewards of the job (pay, promotions) are apparently tied to the latter.

Push back at one of these functionaries and you will quickly be told, "I'm just doing my job. I don't make the rules."

Some of these misguided souls, finding no other satisfaction in their work, get satisfaction (attention?) from exerting petty tyranny over others. Others may be speaking the literal but partial truth when they say, "I'm just doing my job." They should add for the sake of accuracy, ". . . in a way that I perceive that my superiors want it done." Their perceptions may be far from accurate.

In all cases, something positive can be done. For the petty tyrant, one has to find a way to make him glow for performing in the desirable way. (And since this may be hard to do, one may have to fall back on the last-but-not-least alternative: change the job or change the man). For the person who has an inaccurate picture of what his superiors want, there's plainly a need to spell out the true intent, to make sure he knows what is to be done and can recognize when it has been done properly.

Here's a similar example: "We've got to teach that foreman to train his men." (It's the production manager of a manufacturing company speaking.) "Training is his responsibility."

The foreman knew what his men needed to know, all right; but he didn't tell them, and production suffered.

Why didn't he do what needed to be done? What did he get out of keeping his men ignorant?

Status! Anyone who wanted to know what was going on had to talk to the foreman. The foreman was cock of the roost; and, by keeping his subordinates uninformed, he thought he would stay that way. It was more rewarding (in *his* perception) not to perform as expected.

Solution? Not training. Make it matter to perform as desired.

And another example. In one of the large gold mines of Africa, the management once decided that they had a training problem involving African workers who operated the drilling rigs on the mine face. "We've got to teach these men to wear their ear plugs," they said. The discussion with one of the managers went something like this:

"What happens if these men don't wear their ear plugs?"

"Why, they go stone deaf from the unbelievable noise."

"Do they know *how* to wear their ear plugs?"

"Of course. All they have to do is stick them into their ears."

"Do they have the plugs handy?"

"Yes. They carry them in their pocket. As a matter of fact, they are checked when they enter the mine to make sure they *do* have their ear plugs with them."

"I see. So they know how to wear the plugs, and the plugs are always available?"

"That's right. But they don't wear them, and they really should."

"Why?"

"Why, to keep from going deaf, of course. Nobody oughta wanna go deaf."

"Do you have any idea why they *don't* wear their ear plugs?"

"You know why they don't wear their ear plugs? They don't wear their ear plugs because this is the highest job an African can have in this mine . . . and he wears his deafness like a *status symbol*."

Well, that put a new light on the problem. Then it was seen for what it was, a problem where performing as desired wasn't nearly as rewarding as performing otherwise. Loss of hearing was more desirable than loss of status. Notice again that all the training in the world is not likely to get those ear plugs worn.

No doubt you can think of several possible solutions when the problem is posed in this manner: How can management make "being a driller" more visible to the outside world than deafness?

It's a fact that there's a whole world out there just filled with people who are not doing as you would like. Not all are acting against your wishes because they don't know any better or because they don't know how to do differently. Most behave the way they do because they feel that *their* way leads to more favorable consequences for them than does *your* way. If you want them to do differently, you will have to invent a way to reverse things so that your way leads to the rosier results.

Why do you suppose all those people in the prisons of our land don't straighten up and live right when they are released? Certainly they know we *want* them to do so, and many know *how* to do so. They also know it is important to do so if they are to avoid pursuit and arrest. But they don't. Why?

In some way their "contrary" behavior is more rewarding, has more payoff, leads to more desirable outcomes. When the pros and cons (steady there!) are weighed, the cons win out. There may be some undesirable consequences of a life of crime, of course; but, on balance, the advantages must be perceived by the criminal to outweigh the disadvantages.

This is an appropriate point to re-emphasize that problems of this kind do not always fall so neatly into categories as do our examples. Typically, problems have elements of more than one of the categories we have discussed, or they can move from one category to another.

In this chapter we have looked at cases where the consequences of undesired performance were more favorable than those that followed desired performance. Now consider this case. How often, when you have guests, do you rush over to where the kids are playing quietly in the corner and say, "Hey, kids, you're doing a *great* job of playing quietly in the corner"? Or do you, like most of us, wait until they start acting up and *then* rush over to scold?*

One can argue that you are, at best, providing no consequence for desired behavior. There may be favorable results for playing quietly in the corner, but *you* aren't the source of them.

A gloomier view of the situation is this: If *attention from parent* is viewed by your child as desirable, what must he do to get it?

*Our thanks to Lloyd Homme for this example.

When you ignore episodes of peace and quiet but attend to the uproars, you strengthen the likelihood that you will be confronted by an uproar.

An old expression fits here: It's the squeaky wheel that gets the grease. Might not this be why people feel that to get action they must do something other than behave in a manner resembling "sitting quietly in the corner"?

We're not suggesting, by the way, that you "spoil" your children by refraining from admonition when they misbehave. We are only making the point that when you forget to "glow after good" as well as "growl after bad," you run the risk of making the growl a rosier consequence than you intend.

PP: Bob, tell them about the apes at your house.

RFM: What do you mean?

PP: Well, the gibbons live in a cage in the family room, right?

RFM: Right.

PP: And what happens when the family is watching TV that gets you all upset?

RFM: Well, the apes will bang their metal food dish against the screen of their cage. They bang and bang, and make such a racket we can't hear the program.

PP: And?

RFM: And they oughta wanna *not do that.*

PP: What happens when they do it?

RFM: Why, someone gets up and gives them something to eat to shut them up.

PP: So dish banging is followed by food?

RFM: Right. But they oughta wanna not bang their dish *anyhow*. We keep telling them to stop monkeying around . . . but it doesn't seem to do any good.

Even our educational establishment is loaded with examples of conditions or consequences that make someone's world brighter for *not* performing as you wish.

Let's begin with an analogy. Suppose that while walking in the park you come upon a man standing in front of two plants and muttering to himself. He is using a watering can to water one of the plants. You ask him what he is doing.

"I'm trying to make *that* one grow," he replies, and points to the *other* one.

"Well," you might ask, puzzled, "if you want *that* one to grow, why are you watering *this* one?"

"Because it oughta wanna grow anyhow!"

Whacky? Of course. Yet this is very much like the way our school system is operated.

The chief goal of a school is to help students' capabilities grow—to change their state of knowledge, skill, and understanding. Thus, the measure of success is the degree to which the students' capabilities are increased. Since student performance is what is desired, one would think that the rewards of the system (money, raises, position, status) would be strongly tied to the primary reason for its existence. Yet this appears not to be the case. Look at the salary schedule of nearly every school and you will find that the rewards (favorable consequences) of the system have little direct relationship to effective teaching. Raises and promotions are based almost exclusively on the number of months served and the number of academic credit hours earned. There is little or no attempt to tie these rewards (for the teacher) to the quantity and quality of student performance.

In these circumstances, to say that the teacher oughta wanna teach more effectively is to behave like the nut with the sprinkling can; it is demanding one kind of performance while rewarding another.

At the university level, the situation is even more bizarre. Here the professor gets his promotions and raises not on how well he succeeds with students, but on the basis of how much he publishes, how many government grants he is able to garner, and the number of committees on which he serves. Again, he is exhorted to do one thing while being rewarded for another.

Since people tend to do those things that brighten their world, the moral is:

Water the performance you want to grow.

Think for a moment about the expression "resistance to change." It's a judgment often made about people who don't perform as desired. But the expression is misleading, because it puts a derogatory emphasis where it doesn't belong. When people oppose the introduction of some new idea or thing, there usually isn't an *active* resistance in force. Often, people cling to the old because there is *no real reason,* no favorable consequence to *them,* for doing it the new way. It is more comfortable, more pleasant, more rewarding to stay with the old. So here again, simply plying people with information about the new thing or exhorting them that they oughta wanna be in favor of newness may not change much. The desired performance (the new thing) will be more readily adopted (and made to work during any "teething troubles") if it is plain to the doer how it will make his world brighter.

In much the same way, the teacher passes the blame for his own failure to be interesting by complaining about the student's "short attention span." Much better if he approached the problem by asking himself, "What's the consequence to the student if he does pay attention?" If the honest answer is "boredom," then there isn't much doubt where the remedy lies.

One more category can be listed here. Let's call it the "don't-let's stick-our-necks-out-more-than-we-have-to" category. It's found at many levels in the working world and private life, and can be found under at least two subheadings, the mental version and the physical version.

A typical instance of the first is found in the person who apparently "doesn't like to take responsibility." This is often a person who has discovered that when he makes a wrong decision he gets it in the neck. And if he gets it in the neck often enough and hard enough, he's going to conclude that one way of shutting off aversive consequences is to make *fewer* of these decisions. Eventually, he establishes an equilibrium, making as few decisions as it is possible to make without getting genuine complaints that he's loafing.

You can think of your own examples of students who try but get poor grades and children who seem reluctant to do chores.

That's the mental aspect of the problem. The physical aspect is similar. Some activities are physically exacting; the more you do, the more tired you get. When getting excessively tired leads to no positive consequence (in the eyes of the doer, that is), he, too, finds a point of equilibrium.

When someone is exhibiting these symptoms, people may say, "He's a good man, but . . . ." Or, leaping sprightly to conclusions, they judge: "He's not ambitious." "He doesn't care." "He procrastinates." Or worst of all, "He's lazy."

The person judged may not like to act this way. But, as he sees the world, the less he does, the less he has to answer for or the less he suffers. The consequence—or, more accurately in most cases, the sum of the consequences—for doing more was not worth the effort.

Maybe he doesn't have the mental or physical stuff to perform as you would like. But if you're the one in charge of the consequences that come to him as a result of action or non-action, maybe you should take a close look at those consequences to make sure they are worthy of the effort you are expecting.

What to do

Determine whether *non*-performance or *other* performance leads to more favorable consequences than would desired performance.

How to do it

Ask these questions:

- What is the result of doing it his way instead of my way?
- What does he get out of his present performance in the way of reward, prestige, status, jollies?
- Does he get more attention for *mis*behaving than for behaving?
- What event in the world *supports* (rewards) his present way of doing things? (Are you inadvertently rewarding irrelevant behavior while overlooking the crucial behaviors?)
- Is he "mentally inadequate," so that the less he does the less he has to worry about?
- Is he physically inadequate, so that he gets less tired if he does less?

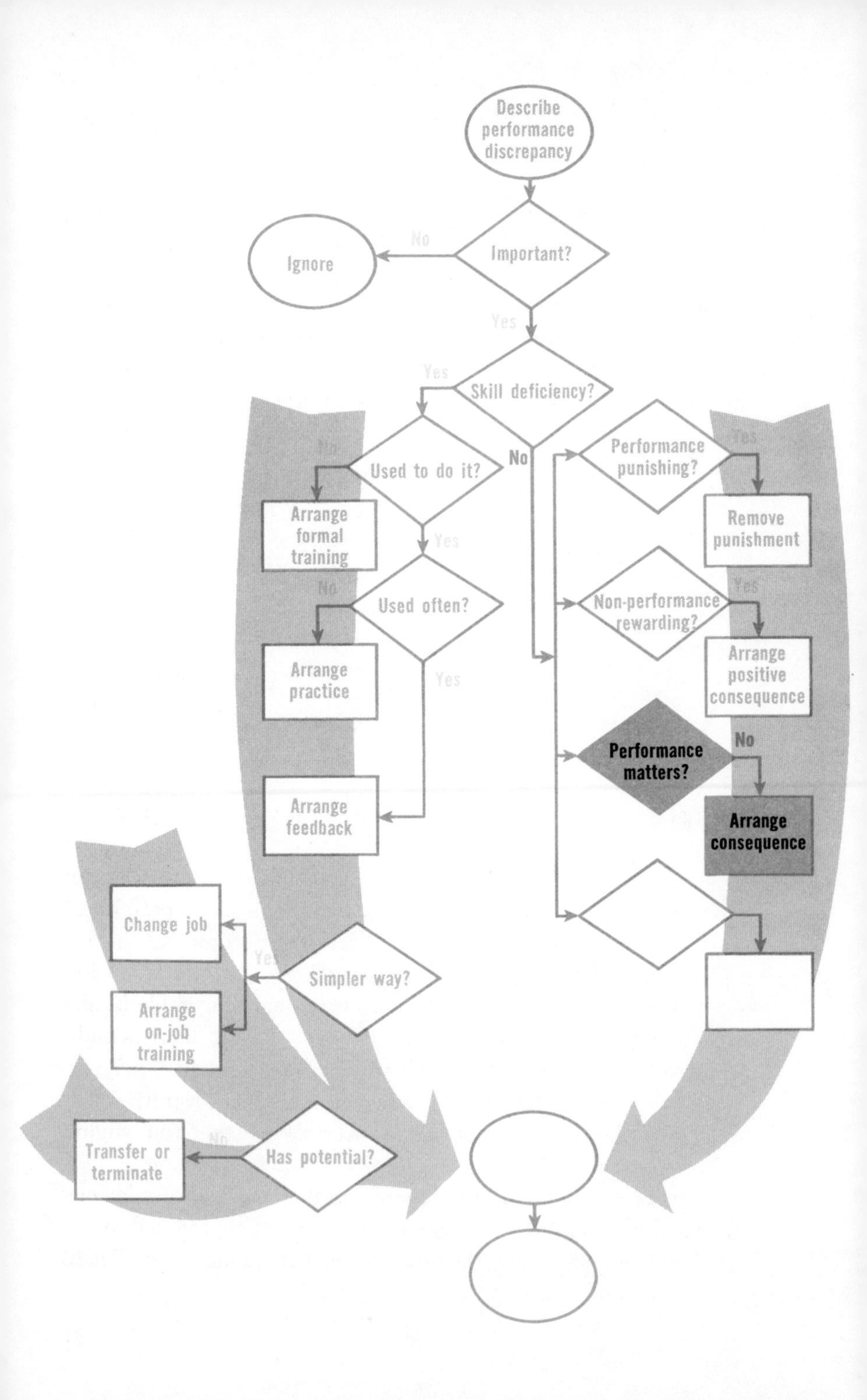

Describe performance discrepancy
Important?
No
Ignore
Yes
Skill deficiency?
Yes
No
Used to do it?
No
Arrange formal training
Yes
Used often?
No
Arrange practice
Yes
Arrange feedback
Performance punishing?
Yes
Remove punishment
Non-performance rewarding?
Yes
Arrange positive consequence
Performance matters?
No
Arrange consequence
Simpler way?
Yes
Change job
Arrange on-job training
Has potential?
No
Transfer or terminate

Does Performing Really Matter?

■ WHERE WE ARE

An important discrepancy is known or suspected not *to be due to a skill deficiency.*

Sometimes a performance discrepancy continues to exist *neither* because the performer doesn't know how to perform *nor* because he isn't motivated, but because it simply doesn't matter whether or not he performs. Nothing happens if he takes the trouble to perform as someone wants; nothing happens if he doesn't.

The laws of behavior tell us that when a performance is not followed at least periodically by an event considered favorable by the performer, that performance will tend to disappear. If there is nothing to make it worth doing, it will tend not to get done.

An important point (because few people seem to grasp it): Wagging your forefinger at someone and telling him, "You oughta wanna," does *not* qualify as a universal incentive to action.

A common instance of this cause of a performance discrepancy comes from that generally unpleasant area known as paperwork. Managers complain, "Reports just don't get in on time," or "Those reports are haphazardly done."

In such instances, the conversation continues like this: "The reports are sloppily done?"

"They certainly are. And they don't come in on time."

"Why not, do you suppose?"

"They just don't seem to care!"

"What happens if the reports are late?"

"Well, then I have to explain to my superiors why I am late with *my* reports."

"No, no. What happens to the person who submits the report?"

"Well, nothing, I guess. But he oughta wanna get them in on time."

"What happens if the reports are sloppily done?"

"Disaster! My poor secretary runs herself ragged trying to get them cleaned up in time to attach to my own report."

"Yes, but what happens to the man who sends in the sloppy work?"

"Well, nothing, I guess."

"You don't phone him or drop him a memo to tell him he has not met expected standards?"

"No."

"You don't send the reports back for *him* to correct?"

"Heavens, no. There's never *time*."

"So it doesn't really matter *to the man* whether his reports are well done and on time?"

"No, I guess not. But he oughta wanna do them right."

Let's not get caught up in a debate about the importance of paperwork. The example is intended to illustrate that desired performance is less likely to be attained when that performance does not matter to the performer, when the perceived consequence is the same to the performer whether he does it right or some other way.

Around 1960, many programmed instruction enthusiasts began exhorting publishers to be concerned about the effectiveness of the books they publish. "From now on you must publish materials that work," they said. "You must test them and modify them until they *do* work." And they added, "You must have the data available to the user so that he can tell exactly what your materials do and how well they do it."

One or two publishers did just that. They went through all the stages, and made available the data describing the effectiveness of the finished product. But after a while there was some backsliding. We vividly remember a discussion with one sincere and dedicated publisher who told us why. "In the period of an entire year," he said, "we had *two* requests from teachers for information about how well the programs work. It was as though nobody cared whether they worked or not. There was just this big silence."

Here again, it simply didn't seem to matter whether the publisher performed as the programming enthusiasts desired. There was no meaningful consequence. It's easy to say the publisher oughta wanna do things according to the state of the art, that it would be the honorable thing to do, or that he ought to get personal satisfaction from doing so. But the reality is that it costs a lot of time and money to refine materials until they do a specific job reliably; and without a meaningful consequence, this kind of effort will likely shrink to a mere trickle of good intention.

Recently a professor of music was exasperated about a discrepancy he noted in his conducting class. "I have a student who just slashes his baton up and down like a kid with a flyswatter. I just can't get him to do it *right*," he told us. After some discussion of the situation he finally said, "No, for him it just doesn't seem to matter. He seems to be able to communicate to the orchestra, and they do everything he wants them to do. But he ought to want to be more elegant when he conducts."

Here is a case of a man who gets results his way that are just as good as if he used the professor's way. Why *should* he change when there doesn't seem to be any real reason to do so (other than for a grade)?

And here's a common "problem" solved by ingenuity. A professor kept urging his students to "sit down front" when attending lectures and demonstrations in the tiered classroom. But students continued to sit in the back. "If you sit in the front," the professor would tell the students, "I won't have to talk so loudly." But they still sat in the back.

Someone finally hit on an idea—it was adopted and the problem was solved. The solution? The first five rows of seats were upholstered; the remaining rows were left with hardwood chairs. Then almost everyone tried to get to class early so they could sit down front.

Meanwhile, nearer home, you have undoubtedly heard your neighbor complain that his offspring simply will not pick up after himself, no matter how often he is told. If you were to listen to a conversation between this parent and someone skilled in the use of our checklist, you might hear:

"He doesn't pick up after himself, even though you've made it clear you expect him to?"

"I've told him and I've told him, but it doesn't do any good."

"And he knows where to put the clothes?"

"Of *course* he does. He isn't stupid, you know."

"Sorry. Ah, tell me, what is the result of his not picking up after himself?"

"The result? The result is that I spend half *my* time picking up after him. *That's* the result!"

"I understand. But what's the result to *him?*"

"I nag."

"And how about if he does pick up?"

"What do you mean?"

"Does something favorable happen if he picks up after himself for a certain period of time—like an extra movie, or a round of applause from the family, or a favorite meal, or something else he might like to have?"

"Certainly *not!* You don't think I'm going to *bribe* him to do something he oughta wanna do anyhow, do you?"

[*Bribe* is a loaded word, carrying a connotation of something illegal or designed to make someone do something against his will, breaking moral laws. But bribery is a concept having to do with ethics rather than with the laws of behavior. What we're talking about is a *positive consequence* that, if you like loaded words, could as well be called a *reward.* By providing a positive consequence, we increase the probability that behavior will occur. Even when we do something we don't like to do (when, say, we submit to surgery), we do it because we expect that life will be improved as a result. But we don't look on "getting better as a result of surgery" as a bribe. When a mother says to her child, "If you pick up your clothes for a week, I'll take you to a movie," it is not bribery. It is the offer of an incentive (a consequence desired by the child) in return for performance desired by the mother.]

In this case, the performance discrepancy is that the youngster doesn't pick up his clothes in the desired manner with the desired regularity. He knows how to do it, but he doesn't do it. Thus, the discrepancy is not likely to be eliminated by training or instruction. His world doesn't get brighter if he does as expected; and, since he's so used to being nagged that he doesn't even hear it, his world doesn't get dimmer if he doesn't. In effect, nothing meaningful happens one way or the other. There is no consequence for performing as desired, so he tends not to.

Again, it is easy to say that he oughta wanna pick up after himself because it is the adult thing, the right thing, the moral thing, the mother-saving thing, etc. And some day, probably, he *will* pick up after himself, because it matters to his self-concept or his convenience to do so. But right now there are none of these *internal* consequences. If you expect him to perform, then, you must see to it that his performance is followed by an *external* consequence that has value *for him.*

Another interesting example is found in the inspection departments of some manufacturing companies. One of the duties is that of inspecting incoming materials. In one such plant, the features to be evaluated include the smoothness of various metal surfaces. The inspector checks to see if the smoothness meets or surpasses specifications. If it does, the material is accepted and sent on to the production department. If not smooth enough, the material is returned to the vendor.

It was noticed that inspectors were rejecting material that was, in fact, smooth enough to be accepted. "We have a training problem," said a manager. "We need to teach these inspectors to be more accurate in their smoothness judgments."

By now you are probably ahead of us and know that training wasn't the solution.

To the question, "What is the consequence of performing as desired?" a double answer appeared. To the inspectors, the result of rejecting a good batch was nothing. The batch went back to the vendor; and the vendor, knowing the game, probably let it sit in his warehouse for a month or so and then resubmitted it. On the other hand, accepting a bad batch brought the wrath of the production department down on an inspector's head.

Thus, there was no noticeable consequence of rejecting a good batch of material (undesirable performance), but it was punishing to accept a bad batch of material (also undesirable performance). The result was that the inspectors, without even realizing it, gradually rejected more and more good batches in order to avoid the punishment that came with accepting a bad one. This was not a conscious action; it just happened.

There are a number of options for correcting this kind of problem. Management could act to make both undesirable alternatives equally undesirable to the inspectors. Since the inspectors *want* to perform well, one could also make the accuracy of their performance more immediately visible to them. If an inspector knew he was making a bad decision, he wouldn't make it. In this case, performance feedback would probably do the trick.

Actually, however, a third alternative was selected, mostly because of the awkwardness and time needed in providing immediate feedback. Since this situation turned out to be a combination of a skill maintenance and a no-consequence problem, a little device was constructed with which the inspectors could periodically check their smoothness perceptions. The device provided a number of graded samples for an inspector to judge, and then told him whether he was right or wrong. He wasn't learning anything he didn't already know, but he *was* keeping his skill sharpened. It would have also helped to equalize the consequence for either of the undesired performances (accepting a bad batch or rejecting a good one), or to have increased the consequence of good performance, but to our knowledge this was not arranged.

As mentioned elsewhere, many discrepancies have elements of more than one cause; this was one such example.

In summary, when you're dealing with a case where it looks as though a person *could* perform if he had to or wanted to, one of the things to look for is the *consequence* of doing it. If there *isn't any*—at least if there isn't any that is considered favorable by the person expected to perform differently—then the remedy that suggests itself is to arrange one.

When you want someone to perform in some particular manner, one rule is:

Make it matter.

What to do

Determine whether there is a meaningful consequence for the desired performance.

How to do it

Ask these questions:

- Does performing as desired matter to the performer?
- Is there a favorable outcome for performing?
- Is there an undesirable outcome for *not* performing?
- Is there a source of satisfaction for performing?
- Is he able to take pride in his performance, as an individual or as a member of a group?
- Does he get satisfaction of *his* needs from the job?

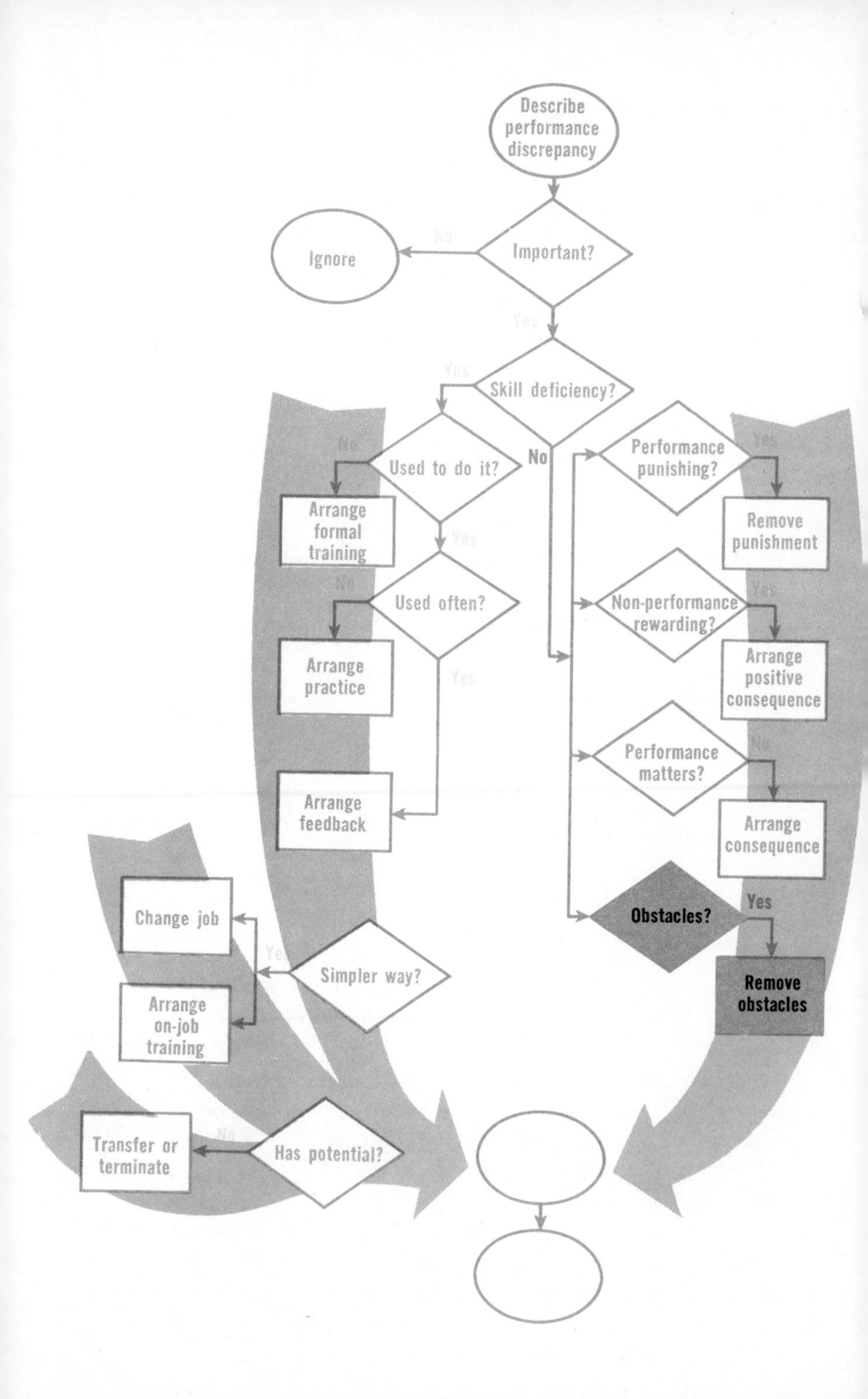

Describe performance discrepancy
Important?
No
Ignore
Yes
Skill deficiency?
Yes
No
Used to do it?
No
Arrange formal training
Yes
Used often?
No
Arrange practice
Yes
Arrange feedback
Performance punishing?
Yes
Remove punishment
Non-performance rewarding?
Yes
Arrange positive consequence
Performance matters?
No
Arrange consequence
Obstacles?
Yes
Remove obstacles
Simpler way?
Yes
Change job
Arrange on-job training
Has potential?
No
Transfer or terminate

CHAPTER 11

Are There Obstacles to Performing?

▪ WHERE WE ARE

An important discrepancy is known or suspected not *to be due to a skill deficiency.*

If he knows how to do it, isn't doing it, but ought to do it, there are four general causes to look for:

1. It's punishing to do it.
2. It's rewarding *not* to do it.
3. It doesn't matter whether he does it.
4. There are obstacles to doing it.

We have discussed the first three; now we'll consider the issue of obstacles.

Have you ever said to yourself, "I could do this job perfectly well if only the &*%$#@%¢ telephone would stop ringing and those idiots next door would stop pestering me so that I could concentrate for five minutes at a time"?

That's a perfect example of a situation in which a job would get done more efficiently if the conditions were changed—without the need for instruction. It's a typical problem for people in all walks of life. The victim would do an acceptable job, if only he could get *at* the job. Some are more stoical about this than others, of course. The lower we are in the pecking order, the more likely it is that we'll tolerate an obstacle, since we are not in the happy position of being able to tell the boss, "Quit bugging me!"

We know that in industry it is courting inefficiency, if not disaster, to organize in a way that gives a man more than one boss. Inevitably it happens that in trying to please one, he must neglect the interests of others. Multiple-bossism is recognized as bad management. Yet in our schools a student has as many bosses as he has teachers, each putting demands upon his time and attention and, frequently, each imposing different rules. When the student fails to meet the demands and follow the rules, unfavorable consequences follow. And eventually the student can end up saying, "I hate school."

Now this is not to say that no student ever goofed off. But it does indicate that we might get more from students (and students might get more satisfaction from school) if we paid more heed to the conditions under which they are expected to perform.

Teachers, too, are prevented from doing a better job by the conditions under which they work. Too often, the teacher is expected to collect milk money, keep interminable records, and otherwise devote considerable time to chores just as well handled at a clerical level. We have talked to teachers in many colleges who are expected to use films, slides, and other visual materials freely. But the equipment and help they need are available only from a remote (but oh-so-central) location, through a flurry of paperwork administered by an office that is not always open for business when the teacher can go there.

Here's another example. Imagine yourself called in by the personnel director of a French department store. He engages you in the following conversation:

"Monsieur, I have a training problem."

"Yes?"

"Oui. I would like you to prepare a programmed instruction course on salesmanship for our sales clerks."

"I see."

"How much will it cost?"

What do you reply? You know that training is a solution, not a problem, and that the personnel director hasn't said a single word about his problem. He has only told you what he has decided on as a solution. (Though it would be a mistake to enter into a discussion of cost at this point, it would be an even bigger mistake to imply that he didn't know what he was talking about or that he has no business talking solutions until he understands the problem.)

What is needed is more information, information that will explain why this man thinks (1) that his employees need sales training and (2) that the training should be in a particular format.

In answer to such questions, the personnel director responded that his concern was triggered by the fact that gross receipts were not what they should be.

Now the amount of money taken in by a store is only partly related to the skill of its sales clerks. Since in further questioning the director said nothing directly related to sales clerks and their abilities, we began to wonder if the cause of the problem might be elsewhere. We asked to be shown around the store. Within a few minutes, we noted several clumps of people gathered around cash registers trying to give the clerks money to complete a transaction. Then we found that some merchandise was placed on the counters according to manufacturer rather than according to type. If you wanted to look at transistor radios, for example, you might first go to the Phillips department to see what they had, and then walk to the Telefunken department (some distance away) to see what they had there.

In some ways, this is typical of the situations wrongly labeled "training problems." Basically, what is wrong is that management has rushed to a solution without first looking at other elements of the problem. Here, as in most situations involving those infinitely variable entities called people, there is probably no perfect solution to yield a perfect answer. But there are usually some solutions that are superior to others in terms of return for effort expended.

It's not too much to say that the management of this store singled out the element that was most visible and most under its control, and made it the scapegoat for an important discrepancy. They then identified a solution that involved changing the sales clerks in some way.

The trouble with premature identification of solutions is that they block off exploration of other problem elements. We tend to say to ourselves, "Well, that's that. We've nailed down what we're going to do. Now let's get on with doing it." Because we feel "We're doing something about it," some of the burden of the problem has been lifted from our shoulders.

It's probably clear, however, that other elements contributed to the store's problem. In studying the procedures, it became plain that the store's policies almost seemed designed to prevent customers from buying or, having once bought, to discourage them from coming back again. It was hard to find what one wanted. It was hard to complete a purchase. Once the sales procedures were revised and the time to complete a transaction was reduced, sales increased.

The training director of a dynamite factory overseas told of an instance where all the training in the world would have been useless in solving the problem.

He was called by a plant manager. "I've got a training problem," said the manager. "These people are lazy. They fall asleep on the job, and they don't come to work regularly. I want you to come up here and teach them their jobs. I want you to teach them to be motivated."

The training director was too smart to fall into the trap of taking a statement like that at face value, especially since it began with the usual confusion of problem with solution. Knowing his human relations, he replied, "I'll come and take a look around so that I can see more clearly what needs to be taught." (It doesn't get you very far to tell a client he is probably wrong in his diagnosis. It works better to agree that he has a problem and then do your analysis out loud, hoping that *he* will spot the difficulty.)

The training director went to the site, looked around, talked to people, and reviewed employee records. All the while, he was asking himself whether he was dealing with a skill deficiency—and, if not, why the men were not performing as expected.

He found the answer in an unexpected place—the medical office. Better than 60 percent of the employees in question were suffering from a disease that shows up in symptoms of sleeping sickness. *Of course* these men were falling asleep on the job. *Of course* their attendance was spotty.

But there wasn't anything wrong with their skill or with their motivation. They were simply sick. Once cured, all was well.

Again, all the training in the world would not have done much good. Had the training director simply done what he was asked, his training program would have failed. Then the plant manager might have said, "Why spend all this money on a training department? We'd be better off without 'em." And what's more, if the training department continually used training as a solution for the wrong problems, he'd be right.

Thus, if performance discrepancies appear *not* to be due to a lack of skill or motivation, one thing to look for is the *obstacle*. "I can't do it" isn't always just an alibi; it can be an accurate description of the situation. And if you will look around to see what might be obstructing performance, you will find the solution to at least some of your performance problems.

Obstacles can take many forms and, as illustrated by the case of the dynamite workers, may appear in unlikely places. A few years ago, one of us was asked to review a division of a company and make whatever recommendations for improvement seemed appropriate. Things were going pretty well, so this was not one of the instances that begins with "I've got a training problem." Production was down a little, but it was not a matter of panic proportions, although puzzling.

As is customary, two or three days were spent soaking in the activities of the division, working from inspectors of incoming material toward the loading dock.

It was learned that though production was sagging, nothing else had changed. There was no new product that people had to learn how to build. The same employees were still on the scene. There were no new, complicated machines to master. There seemed to be no morale or personality problems of any significance. Parts were flowing smoothly to the supply bins. Tools were plentiful and in good working order.

Then what?

The answer, the ridiculous answer, was discovered while sitting with some spot welders at their workbenches. It was noticed that they were rather slow in getting up to refill their empty parts bins. Why? They were one stool short on the production floor! Getting up meant that your stool might be gone when you returned. So each girl dawdled when her bins were empty, and each spent time carving her initials or taping identifying marks on "her" stool.

For want of a stool . . . . Clearly there was an obstacle to desired performance.

And there was the student who was failed on an examination because he left the answer sheet blank. "Your *attitude* is terrible," said the teacher. "Can you give me one good reason why you didn't fill in a single answer on this test?"

"Yes."

"Well?"

"I didn't have a pencil."

Another form of obstacle to desired performance that is seldom identified as such is that of absence of information about what is wanted. If a person doesn't *know* that he is expected to perform in some way, he may fail to do so, even though he knows how to do so. At the risk of offending a small minority, we will generalize that nobody can read minds. If you want someone to perform in a particular way, let him in on the secret. Tell him what is expected, and tell him what the standards are. Note the examples that follow.

The Case of the Secret Agenda

The secret agenda is too common in industry. It often shows up in discussions with the bewildered employee who has just been demoted or booted clear off the payroll.

"What did you do that got you fired?" one might ask.

And you might receive a reply like this: "I don't know! I honestly don't know. My performance reviews were all favorable . . . and my boss kept telling me I was doing a good job. Then, all of a sudden, I was fired. I honestly don't know why."

Although it is probably true that some employees pretend ignorance of the reason for their sudden separation, it would be foolish to assume that all of them are being deceitful. More likely it never occurred to anyone to tell the employee what was expected of him, or perhaps those in charge were not mature enough to inform him of what he was doing to cause the displeasure of the establishment.

The Case of the Hidden Hatchet

A large company recently took a look at its course for management trainees. When the course was analyzed for effectiveness, it was noted that some trainees were let go at the end of instruction even though their technical performance was good or adequate. When we asked why, we were told it was because these trainees manifested some personal characteristics considered inappropriate for an executive.

Had these characteristics ever been brought to the attention of the trainees so that they might have a chance to change them? No. Why not? Because it is hard to tell a man that you don't like the color of his ties or that his nose-scratching is offensive. It is easier to tell him that he is not suitable for the job, or to mumble something about performance, and fire him.

The course now includes a personality checklist that the training supervisor *must* fill out and show the trainees each month. In this way, trainees who exhibit behaviors considered objectionable by management will have an opportunity to change if they so desire.

The Case of the Elusive Evaluation

The faculty of a medical school once complained, "These students of ours will argue for hours over half a point on our written exams. Yet it isn't the *written* exams that are important. We've got to teach them to be less concerned with those darned paper-and-pencil tests." The rest of the conversation went like this.

"The students really care about their performance on the written tests?"

"Yes. And they shouldn't. It's the *subjective* evaluations the staff makes of the students that are important."

"When is this evaluation made?"

"All day and every day our staff members are noting and evaluating each student's actual performance. We note how he performs with patients in the clinic, with other students, and with staff, and how he performs in the lab."

"How do you consolidate the results of these subjective evaluations?"

"We compare notes."

"Who does?"

"The staff. We get together and discuss the progress of each student."

"Is the student present?"

"Certainly not."

"So the results of the written exams are *visible* to the student, but the results of subjective evaluations are *in*visible to him?"

"Yes. But visible or not, it's the subjective evaluations that are really important; and that's what students ought to be interested in."

You can imagine how difficult it was to refrain from asking point-blank, "If they're *that* important, why keep them such a big secret?"

The Case of the Masticating Menace

We met a man highly competent and creative in his field who, we were told, is avoided by friends and business associates alike. Associates dread having to take him along to meet clients if a meal is involved, because he chomps his food with his mouth open—and talks while doing so. He's done it for years, and for years people have avoided taking him to business meals. So far, nobody has had the nerve—or the consideration—to tell him about it.

So why should he change?

How many executives have been fired, kicked upstairs, or retired because their superiors had the position but not the guts to tell them about an offensive but easy-to-correct habit?

How many teachers must there be who return test results to students days, even weeks, after the test was taken, and who then complain that student performance isn't any better than it is—and that the students don't seem to care?

Might your relations with others improve if you could know how they really feel about your present words and actions? Would you be willing to give up using a particular expression, or a gesture, if you knew it was offensive to someone you cared about?

Closely related to not knowing *that* you are expected to do something, is not knowing *when* you are expected to do it. For example, a physical scientist working in the laboratory of a rather large corporation confided that he had been rated down by his boss because of what the boss referred to as an "undesirable characteristic."

"My boss said I didn't know how to keep my mouth shut," complained the scientist.

"And *can* you?" he was asked.

"*Of course* I can. Discretion is the name of the game in the lab I work in. If I couldn't keep my mouth shut, I'd have been out of a job long ago."

"Then what do you suppose the boss is complaining about?"

"Well, every once in a while he calls me into a meeting and asks me to tell them what I *really* think about something or other. And I do."

"And that's bad?"

"Only sometimes. Occasionally there is someone sitting in the meeting from another division, or even from a customer's company, and I'm not aware of it. *Then* when my boss asks what I really think, he seems to want me to say something to make the company look good rather than tell him what I really think. Trouble is . . . I can never tell when to do which."

Thus, if a person is unable to tell *when* to perform in a particular way, if he can't recognize the signal, somebody might conclude that he doesn't know *how*.

In summary, if it looks as though a person knows how to perform but doesn't perform, look for obstacles. Look for things that might be getting in the way of his performing as desired. Look for his lack of authority, lack of time, or lack of tools. Look for poorly placed or poorly labeled equipment. Look for bad lighting and uncomfortable surroundings. Look for lack of *direct* information about *what* to do and *when* to do it. Above all, keep in mind that if he *can* do it but isn't doing it, there is a reason; and only seldom is the reason either a lack of interest or a lack of motivation or desire. Most people want to do a good job. When they don't, it is often because of an obstacle in the world around them.

What to do

Determine whether there are obstacles preventing the desired performance.

How to do it

Ask these questions:

- What prevents him from performing?
- Does he know *what* is expected of him?
- Does he know *when* to do what is expected of him?
- Are there conflicting demands on his time?
- Does he lack the authority?
  ... the time?
  ... the tools?
- Is he restricted by policies or by a "right way of doing it" or "way we've always done it" that ought to be changed?
- Can I reduce interference by improving lighting?
  ... changing colors?
  ... increasing comfort?
  ... modifying the work position?
  ... reducing visual or auditory distractions?
- Can I reduce "competition from the job"—phone calls, "brush fires," demands of less important but more immediate problems?

PART IV

What Should I Do Now?

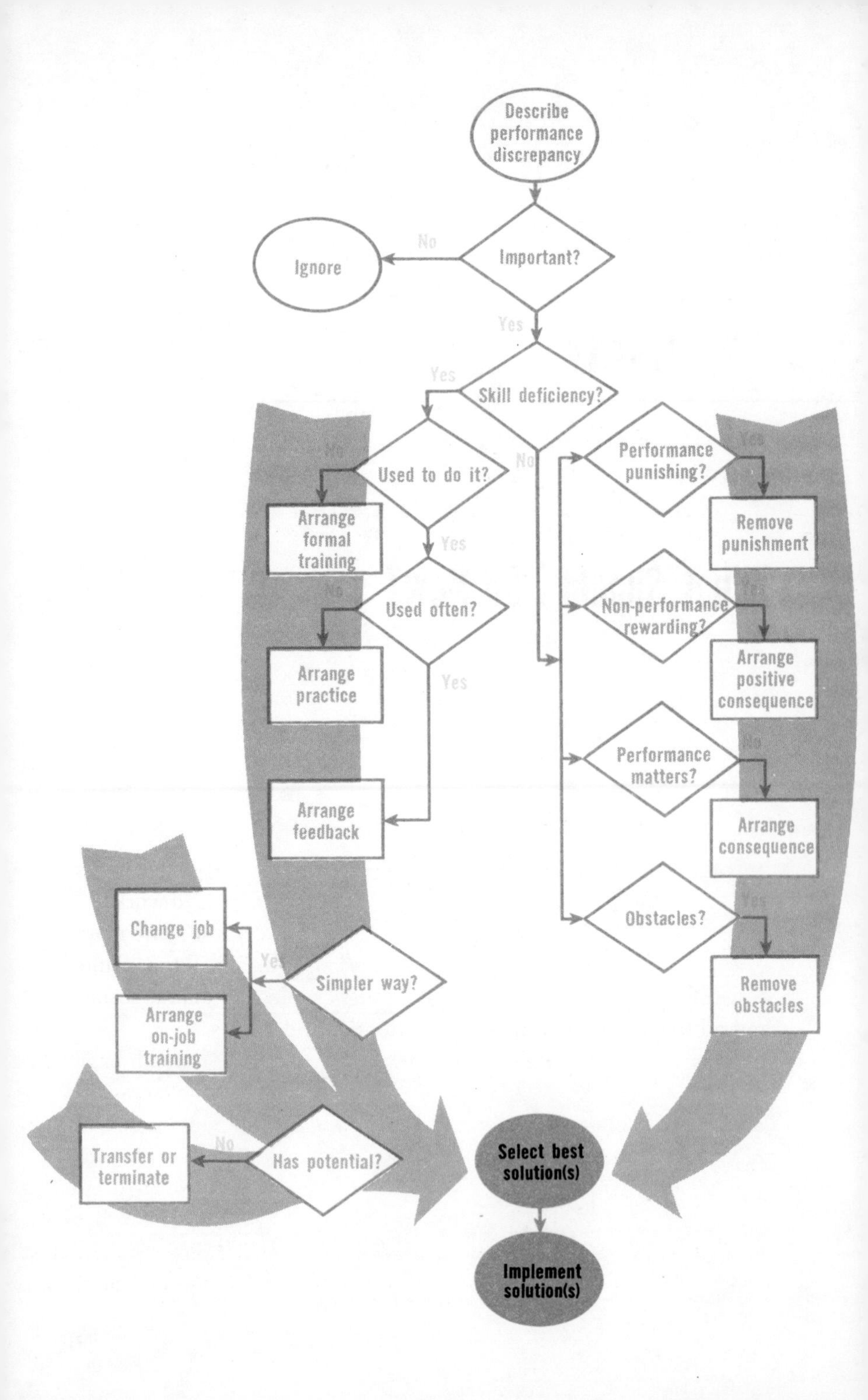

Describe performance discrepancy
Important?
No
Ignore
Yes
Skill deficiency?
Yes
No
Used to do it?
No
Arrange formal training
Yes
Used often?
No
Arrange practice
Yes
Arrange feedback
Performance punishing?
Yes
Remove punishment
Non-performance rewarding?
Yes
Arrange positive consequence
Performance matters?
No
Arrange consequence
Obstacles?
Yes
Remove obstacles
Change job
Simpler way?
Arrange on-job training
Transfer or terminate
No
Has potential?
Select best solution(s)
Implement solution(s)

CHAPTER 12

Which Solution Is Best?

■ WHERE WE ARE

One or more solutions or remedies for a performance discrepancy have been identified.

Isn't this the end of the line? By now you probably have what looks like one or more relevant solutions, so why not put them to work?

It's true you've cleared most of the hurdles, but there's one more question to ponder before racing for the finish line: Will the results be worth the trouble? This can be a tougher question than it seems, and all too often it doesn't get the attention it deserves.

If you have followed the procedure we've described, you'll have concentrated on finding solutions that are *related* to a problem, without too much regard for whether the solution is the most practical or feasible in your situation. As a result, one or more of the remedies you have generated may be inappropriate simply because they are beyond the resources you can bring to bear. Perhaps it's plain that you would not be able to get the money, perhaps it violates policy, or maybe you don't have the organizational "muscle" to implement it.

So, as the first step in deciding which solution is best, ask these questions:

- Are the possible solutions clearly inappropriate or impossible to implement?
- Are the possible solutions plainly beyond our resources?

If the answer to either of these questions is affirmative, you can drop the proposed solutions immediately. If one or more solutions survive this first, gross screening, you can take a closer look at their merits to get an answer to the next question: Is it worth it? These are the questions you'll have to ask to get your answer:

- What would it "cost" to go ahead with the solution?
- What would be the added "value" if I did?

This makes it sound as though we are talking only about money. Not so. We put quotation marks around "cost" and "value" because they both have dimensions other than monetary.

This is not to set aside the usefulness and importance of money as a measuring instrument or limitation in this situation. After all, if you can't afford a particular solution, or if a solution costs more than the results are likely to be worth, plainly there is some analyzing to be done. A less obvious case, perhaps, is that of doing nothing. The cost of the solution should be weighed against the cost of maintaining the status quo. What looks at first like an "unreasonable" cost may look considerably more attractive if the true cost of the present situation is examined.

There's a tendency to say that an existing state of affairs "costs nothing" and that any solution that entails added outlay of money therefore has to be more expensive. But the "hidden cost" of "doing nothing" about a performance discrepancy can be considerable—in inefficient performance, overly long or unnecessary courses, scrap piles larger than they need be, lost or angry customers, employee turnover and absenteeism, and varying degrees of frustration.

Recently, the trainers of a large corporation spent more than a hundred thousand dollars in the development and validation of a single course; a very expensive solution, indeed. But *too* expensive? Hardly. The new course is only *one-fifth* the length of the old one, and it turns out men who can perform better than former graduates. The invested dollars are repaid several times over each year.

But money is only one form of "cost." Implementing a solution may take time, talent, people, dedication, hard work, and so on; and the sum total of the requirement may not be worth the results.

Consider, for example, the parents who feel it important that their offspring play a musical instrument. The visible discrepancy between what is desired and what exists is the degree of musical skill. The solution is "music lessons."

But if we consider the magnitude of the solution, we find it takes more than music lessons to satisfy the discrepancy. There will need to be practice—lots of it—if the discrepancy is to be substantially reduced. There will be a need for money, not only for lessons, but for the instrument. And there is also the wear and tear that may be required to fan practice into the regular activity it needs to be. (The potential extent of this effort can be evaluated only by one who knows the nature of the individual involved and his musical talent. If the potential musician is already very interested, or if he moves in an environment that causes him to want to learn music, or if he has a substantial endowment of talent, there may be no great need of practice-encouraging activity. If, on the other hand, he is disinterested, recalcitrant, untalented, or highly motivated in some *other* direction, it might take a major effort to keep the practice at a desirable level.)

Here we have an example of a "training problem" in which the cost is not just a financial outlay. We must also include the effort needed to get Junior to practice, to convey him to and from lessons, and so on. The question, "What would it cost to go ahead with the solution?" may have opened up some other problem areas.

The situation is similar for the second question you must ask to find out if a solution is worth it (What would be the added value if I did?). It, too, may raise other questions, quite possibly leading to a different view of the problem (and hence to different solutions).

Suppose that our potential musician is a member of a "musical family." The apparent problem is to change the child's musical competence. That's the visible part of the problem, and might be presented as "He oughta wanna learn music, because it will give him a pleasurable skill." But problems can be like icebergs; their bulk may be below the surface. The hidden value–perhaps unspoken, and maybe not even recognized–could be "He oughta wanna learn music, because it is a family tradition that we're proud of, and because it will allow us to continue to talk about music and to continue that valued tradition." In such a case, the musical skill developed by the potential musician is almost incidental to the need of other family members to include him as one of the in-group. Thus, though the discrepancy may truly be stated as lack of musical skill, it also includes the difference between what the family has and what it wants in the way of communication and shared interests with the potential musician.

If the potential musician is disinterested, we must include in our decision-making not only the more obvious issues, but also a judgment as to how far pride in the family tradition makes us willing to work at stimulating the child's lagging interest. It may not be worth the effort (and the cost in family alienation) to try to eliminate the discrepancy.

A home example was used here to show how hard it is to put a firm value on either the magnitude of a discrepancy or the total effort needed in applying the solution. But these imponderables occur in other walks of life, too.

Business has to ask itself whether it should provide management development courses and, if it does, who should take part. And in recent years there has been emphasis on providing enrichment training for the hitherto "unemployable." These are difficult areas in which to decide "Is it worth it?"

School districts, under mounting financial pressure, face the same problems in deciding methods and priorities for revising curricula to meet the demands of a fast-changing world. Teachers, urged to innovate, often must devote a large amount of their own time to developing new ideas—knowing that if they fail they will get stomped on, and that if they succeed they will probably get little recognition. They find it hard to answer the question "Is it worth it?"

If you have compared the solution with the discrepancy and found it to be feasible or practical, fine. That's the end of the road as far as we're concerned here, since your problems are now problems of implementation and not problems of analysis. But what happens if all potential solutions were rejected because they were plainly beyond your resources or because, on close examination, they proved unfeasible or impractical?

The answer is the same for both. You will have to re-examine the problem and the solution to see if one or both can be scaled down. Ask:

- Can the problem be attacked in parts?
- Can a portion of the solution be used to solve a portion of the problem?

Sometimes it makes good sense to settle for less than the ultimate solution. If you shoot for something less than perfection, you may be able to get acceptable results for a good deal less effort. Or, when problems and solutions seem out of reach, it often makes sense to ask: What will give us the most result for the least effort? Which aspect are we best equipped to tackle? Which part of the problem interests us most? Which part of the problem is the most "visible" to those who must be pleased? So . . .

- If you can't afford to train fifty men, can you train five and have them provide on-the-job training for their colleagues?
- If you can't afford to hire all the guards indicated for plant security, can you shore things up sufficiently with closed-circuit TV?
- If you don't have room in the house for a piano, could your child learn to play the piccolo?
- If you don't have the room or the teachers in your school to provide vital vocational training, can you persuade local industry to provide some space and know-how?

- If you can't provide the service to *all*, can you find a quick way to tell who needs the service most?
- If you can't find a foolproof way of telling whether ammunition is in working order other than by firing it, can you use a random sampling technique that will be almost as good?

In summary, once a remedy is found for a performance discrepancy, it is worth thinking about whether the remedy is worth the probable results. To do so will help select which of several remedies may be the most practical, economical, easiest to use—the one most likely to give the most result for the least effort.

What to do

Compare the size of the remedy with the size of the discrepancy.

How to do it

Ask these questions:

- Are any solutions inappropriate or impossible to implement?
- Are any solutions plainly beyond our resources?
- What would it "cost" to go ahead with the solution?
- What would be the added "value" if I did?
- Is it worth doing?
- Which remedy is likely to give us the most result for the least effort?
- Which are we best equipped to try?
- Which remedy interests us most? (Or, on the other side of the coin, which remedy is most visible to those who must be pleased?)

PART V

A Quick-reference Checklist

Now that the steps of our performance analysis are familiar to you, we can give them to you in a quick-reference checklist. Use the checklist as a guide, or as a way to help someone else see why he really oughta wanna re-evaluate the solution he has already decided upon.

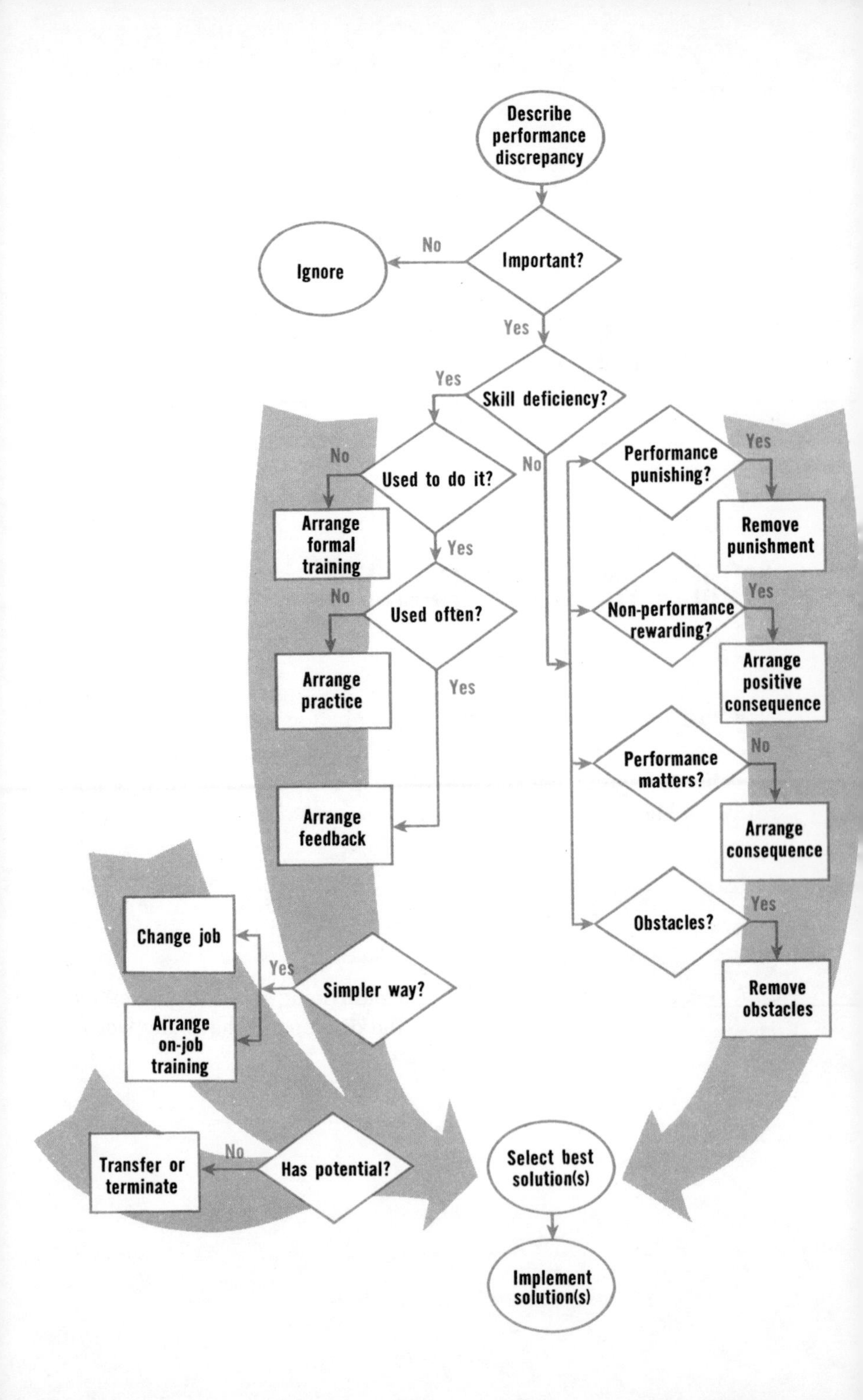

Describe performance discrepancy
Important?
No
Ignore
Yes
Skill deficiency?
Yes
No
Used to do it?
No
Arrange formal training
Yes
Used often?
No
Arrange practice
Yes
Arrange feedback
Performance punishing?
Yes
Remove punishment
Non-performance rewarding?
Yes
Arrange positive consequence
Performance matters?
No
Arrange consequence
Obstacles?
Yes
Remove obstacles
Simpler way?
Yes
Change job
Arrange on-job training
Has potential?
No
Transfer or terminate
Select best solution(s)
Implement solution(s)

Quick-reference Checklist

Key Issues	Questions To Ask
I. He isn't doing what he should be doing. *I think I've got a training problem.*	
1. What is the performance discrepancy?	Why do I think there is a training problem? What is the difference between what is being done and what is supposed to be done? What is the event that causes me to say that things aren't right? Why am I dissatisfied?
2. Is it important?	*Why* is the discrepancy important? What would happen if I left the discrepancy alone? Could doing something to resolve the discrepancy have any worthwhile result?
3. Is it a skill deficiency?	Could he do it if he really had to? Could he do it if his life depended on it? Are his present skills adequate for the desired performance?

Key Issues	Questions To Ask
II. Yes. It is a skill deficiency. *He couldn't do it if his life depended on it.*	
4. Could he do it in the past?	Did he once know how to perform as desired? Has he forgotten how to do what I want him to do?
5. Is the skill used often?	How often is the skill or performance used? Does he get regular feedback about how well he performs? Exactly how does he find out how well he is doing?
6. Is there a simpler solution?	Can I change the job by providing some kind of job aid? Can I store the needed information some way (written instructions, checklists) other than in someone's head? Can I show rather than train? Would informal (i.e., on-the-job) training be sufficient?
7. Does he have what it takes?	Could he learn the job? Does he have the physical and mental potential to perform as desired? Is he over-qualified for the job?

Key Issues	Questions To Ask
III. It is not a skill deficiency. *He could do it if he wanted to.*	
8. Is desired performance punishing?	What *is* the consequence of performing as desired? Is it punishing to perform as expected? Does *he* perceive desired performance as being geared to penalties? Would his world become a little dimmer (to him) if he performed as desired?
9. Is *non*-performance rewarding?	What is the result of doing it his way instead of my way? What does he get out of his present performance in the way of reward, prestige, status, jollies? Does he get more attention for *mis*behaving than for behaving? What event in the world *supports* (rewards) his present way of doing things? (Are you inadvertently rewarding irrelevant behavior while overlooking the crucial behaviors?) Is he "mentally inadequate," so that the less he does the less he has to worry about? Is he physically inadequate, so that he gets less tired if he does less?

Key Issues	Questions To Ask
10. Does performing really matter?	Does performing as desired matter to the performer? Is there a favorable outcome for performing? Is there an undesirable outcome for *not* performing? Is there a source of satisfaction for performing? Is he able to take pride in his performance, as an individual or as a member of a group? Does he get satisfaction of *his* needs from the job?
11. Are there obstacles to performing?	What prevents him from performing? Does he know *what* is expected of him? Does he know *when* to do what is expected of him? Are there conflicting demands on his time? Does he lack the authority? . . . the time? . . . the tools? Is he restricted by policies or by a "right way of doing it" or "way we've always done it" that ought to be changed?

Key Issues	Questions To Ask
	Can I reduce interference by improving lighting? . . . changing colors? . . . increasing comfort? . . . modifying the work position? . . . reducing visual or auditory distractions?
	Can I reduce "competition from the job" – phone calls, "brush fires," demands of less important but more immediate problems?
IV. What should I do now?	
12. Which solution is best?	Are any solutions inappropriate or impossible to implement?
	Are any solutions plainly beyond our resources?
	What would it "cost" to go ahead with the solution?
	What would be the added "value" if I did?
	Is it worth doing?
	Which remedy is likely to give us the most result for the least effort?
	Which are we best equipped to try?
	Which remedy interests us most? (Or, on the other side of the coin, which remedy is most visible to those who must be pleased?)

Epilogue

We have described in this book a way of analyzing a particular kind of problem—that of human performance. Though it may seem to have taken a long time to describe it, it doesn't take long to *use* it. The procedure, after all, represents a way of thinking about things; and, after a little practice, you will find yourself quickly ticking your mental way through the key questions. In just a few seconds you will be able to see a problem in a new light—and then point to a solution that's likely to work.

If you analyze *your* performance problems systematically, you may even come to view some of the larger problems of the world from a new vantage point and understand why some of the "tried and true" solutions are so ineffective. You may, for example, find new ways of thinking and responding to such comments as:

"Traffic deaths can be reduced through education."
"Teachers really oughta wanna teach better."
"Doctors really oughta wanna work in ghettos."
"Industry really oughta wanna pollute less."
"Kids really oughta wanna have more respect for their parents."
"People oughta wanna have fewer children."

Our checklist won't help you to understand *everything* about why people behave as they do. Nothing will do that . . . yet. But if each of us could perceive more clearly the nature of just *one* important human problem—and throw his weight behind a solution *related* to the cause, we might just move bigger and more important things than mountains.

It's worth trying.

Reprisal!

Every book should have a little corner from which authors are allowed to strike back. After all, several dozen individuals have had a go at our thoughts and at our manuscript—picking and probing, suggesting this, trampling on that, or just staring blankly at a mangled explanation they really should have understood.

Such knavery cannot go unsung—so sing we will. We wave the banner of acclaim for all those who so patiently allowed themselves to be battered by earlier, more primitive explanations of the concepts presented herein, and who were magnanimous enough to batter back.

More pointedly, we skewer with the lance of laud and commendation these generous souls who took pains to try on one or another of our later drafts and tell us just where it pinched and how the fit could be improved: John McCann, Rodney Cron, Randy Mager, Maryjane Rees, Vernon Rees, Andy Stevens, Walter Thorne, and Tom Watts.

Long may they dangle!

Robert F. Mager
Peter Pipe

For Your Further Reading . . .

BRETHOWER, KAREN S. "Maintenance Systems: The Neglected Half of Behavior Change." Chapter 3 of *Managing the Instructional Programming Effort,* edited by G. A. Rummler, J. P. Yaney, and A. W. Schrader. Ann Arbor, Mich.: Univ. of Michigan Press, 1967.

FORD, ROBERT N. "The Obstinate Employee," *Psychology Today,* Vol. 3, No. 6, November, 1969, pp. 32–35.

GILBERT, T. F. "Praxeonomy: A Systematic Approach to Identifying Training Needs." *Management of Personnel Quarterly,* Vol. 6, No. 3, 1967, pp. 20–33.

HARLESS, J. H. "Deriving an Instructional Unit's Objectives." In *Performance Problem Solving Workshop.* Falls Church, Va.: J. H. Harless Co., 1969.

WARREN, MALCOLM W. *Training for Results.* Reading, Mass.: Addison-Wesley Publishing Co., 1969, pp. 47–58.

Also by Robert F. Mager...

Preparing Instructional Objectives, Second Edition is a fully revised version of this influential book. It identifies ways to recognize the characteristics of well-stated objectives and prepares readers to develop original objectives of their own. The new practice materials will help newcomers to the field master the techniques of drafting objectives. If you found the first edition useful, the second edition will be indispensable.

Quick-reference Checklist from **Analyzing Performance Problems** is available in expanded worksheet form, with space for answers to questions. Professionals will find this worksheet a handy tool, especially in interview situations.

Performance Analysis Poster of the flow diagram from *Analyzing Performance Problems* is available as a large (23″ x 35″) 2-color poster.

Measuring Instructional Intent or **Got a Match?** shows how to select or create test items that match the intent of your objectives. The author tells you how to find out whether your instruction is successful. He describes a procedure and offers examples and practice with it that will help you make that critical match between objectives and the test items by which the achievement of those objectives may be measured. Includes an Objective/Item Checklist and Flowchart to use in checking test items.

Goal Analysis explains a procedure that will help you describe the meaning of the goals you hope to achieve—whether these goals deal with attitudes, appreciations, or understandings—so that you will be able to make better decisions toward their achievement and recognize progress and success. The goal analysis procedure is often critical in the development of meaningful and *achievable* objectives.

New by George S. Odiorne...

Management by Objectives II, A System of Managerial Leadership for the Eighties is a complete revision of the classic *Management by Objectives.* The evolution and growth of MBO since the first edition was published in 1965 is the underlying thrust of this second edition. It spells out the fundamental nature of MBO as a managerial system—not an addition to the manager's job—but rather a way of managing. There is more about research into MBO method included in this book—a reflection of the considerable growth of MBO into the dominant form of management in large corporations and government. There is more on applications and implementation, because there is more experience to draw from. The major target for this book is the industrial and business executive, and the governmental, educational, and hospital administrator.

FEARON·PITMAN PUBLISHERS, INC., Belmont, California